Sacred Heart of Jesus

THE
Enthronement
OF THE
Sacred Heart
of Jesus

Edited and published under the direction of

His Eminence Raymond Leo Cardinal Burke

Archbishop Emeritus of Saint Louis

Prefect of the Supreme Tribunal of the Apostolic Signatura

Revised edition
Copyright © 2010 by Marian Catechist Apostolate
United States of America

To purchase copies of this book, please contact:

Marian Catechist Apostolate
La Crosse, Wisconsin
USA
www.MarianCatechist.com

CONTENTS

FOREWORD

DEVOTION TO THE
Sacred Heart of Jesus

Introduction

Devotion to the Sacred Heart of Jesus is a most effective means of living always in the company of Our Lord Jesus Whom we receive in Holy Communion. It consists of an ardent love for Our Lord in the Holy Eucharist with grief at seeing Him so little honored, and it includes acts of reparation for the contempt and offenses committed against Him. Our devotion to the Sacred Heart of Jesus is an extended act of love for Him Who shows us the greatest possible love by offering His Body and Blood for us in the Eucharistic Sacrifice.

In His fourth apparition to Saint Margaret Mary Alacoque, Our Lord revealed His Sacred Heart, declaring: "Behold this Heart which has so loved men that It spared nothing, even going so far as to exhaust and consume Itself, to prove to them Its love. And in return I receive from the greater part of men nothing but ingratitude, by the contempt, irreverence, sacrileges and coldness with which they treat Me in this Sacrament of Love. But what is still more painful to Me is that even souls consecrated to Me are acting in this way" (*Devotion to the Sacred Heart*, p. xxvii).

When the devotional life is neglected, there follows a loss of gratitude and reverence, and a coldness before Our Lord in the Eucharist. Our Lord asked Saint Margaret Mary to make known His desire for a renewed devotion to His Sacred Heart so that He might give His love ever more abundantly, and that we might respond with gratitude, returning our love for His divine love.

The Center of Devotion to the Sacred Heart

The center of devotion to the Sacred Heart of Jesus is the Enthronement of an image of the Sacred Heart in the home. The enthroned image of the Sacred Heart, which may be a picture or a statue, expresses Christ's true Kingship, daily reminding each member of the family to follow in His royal way by making reparation for sins committed and by striving to serve God and neighbor more lovingly.

By the Enthronement of the Sacred Heart, we link the tabernacle of our parish church to our home, inviting Our Lord to be our constant and most intimate Companion. The Enthronement is a way of life. It means that Christ is King of our hearts, and that we desire Him to be present with us always. By the Enthronement, we signify our desire to make our hearts and our homes holy, to sanctify our lives in every aspect.

The Enthronement and Single Persons

Here it should be noted that the Enthronement can be made in every home. Often, in speaking of the Enthronement, I refer to the family, but it is understood that the home may be of a single person. The person living alone, no less than a family household, rightly desires that Christ be his or her constant Companion. Also, there is always a relationship with others (family, friends, colleagues and co-workers) which is expressed in the Enthronement, even by the person who lives alone.

The Enthronement and the Transformation of Society

The practice of the Enthronement of the Sacred Heart of Jesus in the home was begun by Father Mateo Crawley-Boevey, SS.CC. (1875-1961), the great *Apostle of the Enthronement*. Father Crawley-Boevey's work was first confirmed and blessed by Pope Saint Pius X in 1907, and then by every Pope since. When the Holy Father heard of the Enthronement, he told Father Crawley-Boevey directly: "To save the family is to save society. The work you are undertaking is a work of social salvation. Consecrate your life to it." Father Crawley-Boevey could not mistake the important role attributed to this Apostolate by the Holy Father.

Father Crawley-Boevey insisted on the *official* and *social* recognition of the rule of the Sacred Heart of Jesus over the Christian family. The Enthronement is social because Christ's Kingship involves every member of the household in which we live and all our relationships with others, inside and outside the home. Those who carry out the Enthronement inevitably comment on the difference it makes in the relationships of family members with one another and with others.

The Enthronement is also official, in so far as it is the outward expression of an interior commitment to submit one's whole life in obedience to Christ. It is an expression of our acceptance of Him as King of our hearts, and as our constant Companion and Friend. By means of the Enthronement, the grace of the Eucharist extends into the Christian home and, from the Christian home, to the whole world, so that what the saintly Roman Pontiff declared to Father Crawley-Boevey in 1907 remains true in our time. If the company of Christ is cultivated in our homes, His company will be cultivated in every sector of life for the transformation of our society and our world into a civilization of love.

The Enthronement and Consecration

The Enthronement includes necessarily our Consecration to the Sacred Heart of Jesus. The Enthronement without the Consecration would simply amount to the placing of a sacred image in a prominent place in the home. It would be a good and pious practice, but it would not transform lives in the way that the Enthronement, together with the Consecration, does. The Consecration is a "setting apart," a formal dedication of oneself to the Sacred Heart of Jesus. It involves a total offering of oneself to Him, along with the promise of fidelity in the future.

The *Act of Consecration* (page 40) gives expression to the profound meaning of enthroning the image of the Sacred Heart in the home. By the words of Consecration, we articulate the meaning of the Enthronement. We place our hearts totally into the Sacred Heart of Jesus, and we beg Him to be the source of our healing and strength, the medicine and nourishment by which our poor and wounded hearts are made strong and whole. The enthroned image of the Sacred Heart gives us the occasion to renew frequently, throughout the day, our *Act of Consecration*.

The words of the *Act of Consecration* proclaim the reign of the Sacred Heart of Jesus in the heart of each member of the household and in the home itself. The words express the commitment of the family members to return love to the Sacred Heart of Jesus in response to the constant and immeasurable love which He shows us in and through His Church. The *Act of Consecration* pledges frequent reception of Holy Communion, penance for sins committed and acceptance of the Divine Will at death. In short, it is a full response to the twelve promises given by Our Lord to Saint Margaret Mary (page 10).

The Enthronement and the Immaculate Heart of Mary

The Consecration to the Sacred Heart of Jesus is made through the Immaculate Heart of Mary, for the Blessed Virgin Mary remains for us always our Advocate before God, and the Mediatrix of the abundant outpouring of His grace from the Heart of Jesus. Since the Enthronement is made in accord with her maternal example and through her intercession, it is altogether fitting that the faithful consecrate themselves to the Immaculate Heart of Mary and install her image at the time of the Enthronement of the Sacred Heart of Jesus. As the Mother of God stood faithfully at the foot of the Cross, permitting her Immaculate Heart to be spiritually pierced because of her total union with the Sacred Heart of Jesus, so she draws us to enthrone the image of the Sacred Heart in our homes and to consecrate our hearts, one with her Immaculate Heart, to the Sacred Heart of her Son.

Raymond Leo Cardinal Burke
Archbishop Emeritus of Saint Louis
Prefect of the Supreme Tribunal of the Apostolic Signatura

SUMMARY OF THE
Promises of the Sacred Heart

Our Lord made the following twelve promises to Saint Margaret Mary Alacoque for those who honor His Sacred Heart:

1. I will give them all the graces necessary for their state of life.

2. I will give peace in their families.

3. I will console them in all their troubles.

4. They shall find in My Heart an assured refuge during life and especially at the hour of death.

5. I will pour abundant blessings on all their undertakings.

6. Sinners shall find in My Heart the source and infinite ocean of mercy.

7. Tepid souls shall become fervent.

8. Fervent souls shall speedily rise to great perfection.

9. I will bless the homes in which the image of My Sacred Heart shall be exposed and honored.

10. I will give to priests the power to touch the most hardened hearts.

11. Those who propagate this devotion shall have their name written in My Heart, and it shall never be effaced.

12. The all-powerful love of My Heart will grant to all those who shall receive Holy Communion on the First Friday of nine consecutive months the grace of final repentance; they shall not die under My displeasure, nor without receiving their Sacraments; My Heart shall be their assured refuge at that last hour.

CHAPTER 1

THE ENTHRONEMENT OF THE
Sacred Heart of Jesus

The Enthronement of the Sacred Heart of Jesus is a devotional practice wherein an image of the Sacred Heart is enthroned in a prominent place in the home. It is also praiseworthy when carried out in a church, school, business or other area of human activity. The Enthronement, along with the Consecration to the Sacred Heart of Jesus through the Immaculate Heart of Mary, publicly proclaims the rule of the Heart of Jesus over the persons and activities of the place. It is an act of reparation for offenses committed against His Heart and, by the *Act of Consecration*, a pledge to honor the Sacred Heart now and in the future.

Understanding the Enthronement
The Enthronement of the visible image of Our Lord represents our interior commitment to love and obey Him. In his book, *Jesus King of Love*, Father Mateo Crawley-Boevey helps us to understand the Enthronement: "By means of the Enthronement, Jesus really enters the home to have a part in and guide the whole life of the family. His love becomes the soul of both parents and children and His Heart their shrine" (p. 130).

"In the home which acclaims the Heart of Jesus as its King of Love, the Enthronement ought to be the beginning of a *new life*, far more intimate in faith and much more ardent in charity…. This means sharing our family life with Jesus to Whom a throne has been offered precisely in order that He may remain and abide with His friends, blessing everything in the house from dawn to twilight and from the cradle to the grave. How much easier it is to live and struggle, to keep a bright face in spite of our sorrows, when Jesus is the center of the beloved home, when He presides over it as a Friend, Confidant and King. Everything is ennobled and sanctified in this enviable Bethany because Jesus shares the family joys and sorrows. *He really lives* in such a home, and the family lives by Him and with Him" (p. 141).

Blessings from the Enthronement

When we wholeheartedly invite Jesus into our homes and enthrone Him as our faithful Friend and loving King, the true Head of our family, we receive many blessings. Father Crawley-Boevey explains that, "when Jesus crosses the threshold of your home He will say to you, 'Peace be to this house and to all who dwell therein.' Because you have carried out His divine request to be invited to your home, He keeps His promise to bless your family and all its undertakings, to sanctify your joys and sorrows, to console you in all your trials, to keep your family united and to give to it true peace and happiness" (p. 136).

Living the Enthronement and Consecration

Father Francis Larkin, SS.CC., who succeeded Father Crawley-Boevey in the promotion of the Enthronement of the Sacred Heart of Jesus, describes what it means to live daily the Consecration to the Sacred Heart of Jesus and to express the Kingship of Christ in our hearts and in our homes. In his book, *Enthronement of the Sacred Heart*, Father Larkin explains that, by the acts of Enthronement and Consecration, the family is saying, in effect, "Lord, we want You to rule over our family; we adore You as our King of Love; we accept You as our loving Friend, always occupying the first place in our hearts and in our home" (p. 65).

The image of the Sacred Heart visibly represents the Headship of Jesus in the home; the place of enthronement becomes the "holy place" where we gather for daily prayer or whenever help is needed. Jesus is present in our home with us; He is our constant Friend and Guest, ready to help us at any moment. Indeed, He has promised that, "where two or three are gathered in My name, there am I in the midst of them" (*Matthew* 18:20).

The two most important aspects of the Enthronement are Christ's *Kingship* and His *Friendship*. As King and Head of the home, Christ takes His rightful place of authority. He guides and watches over everyone and over every activity. The father, who is head of his family, turns to Christ for wisdom and guidance in making the best decisions as he strives to meet the needs of his children, support his wife, and love all who visit the home. With great humility, he welcomes Christ as Head of his family, the *domestic Church*. As a loyal subject of Jesus, he leads his family in prayer and frequent reception of the Sacraments, and in faithfully following the laws of the Church. The mother, like Mary, also turns to Christ as Head. In a spirit of humility and obedience, she asks Christ for the grace to be a good wife and for the grace to guide her children so that they may grow in holiness. As a result, the children learn to turn to Christ, asking for the grace they need to be obedient to their parents and to live in conformity with His will. Children growing up in a home that witnesses to Christ as the center and King of the family will naturally carry Christ's Kingship into their own future families.

Growing in Love for the Sacred Heart

Our Lord showed Saint Margaret Mary His Heart as a sign of the great love He has for us. He said to her, "Behold this Heart which has loved men so much." When we see His Heart, we are to be reminded that God is love, and that He desires our love in return. While enthroning the Sacred Heart and keeping His Commandments publicly acknowledges His Kingship and Headship, striving to love Him more and more each day is necessary if we are to preserve and deepen our friendship with Him. Frequent participation in the Holy Sacrifice of the Mass and the worthy reception of our King in the Holy Eucharist are particularly fruitful means of deepening our love for and friendship with Christ.

Praying together as a family, sharing with Him the joys and sorrows which form the common experience of all families, and turning to Christ frequently throughout the course of the day to offer little aspirations such as "Sacred Heart of Jesus, I love You" or "Sacred Heart of Jesus, I trust You" help to renew our zeal for living a life for Christ. *The Daily Prayer to the Sacred Heart* is in itself a renewal of one's Consecration. Many families choose to pray this prayer together at some point during the day; for example, each night at mealtime or after praying the family rosary. It is important, however, to renew periodically the *Act of Consecration* on First Fridays, on special days such as anniversaries or birthdays, or even during times of sickness or death.

Living the Enthronement and Consecration to the Sacred Heart of Jesus is a generous and fitting response to His great love for us. In this way, we continually welcome Christ as King, Friend and true Head of the home.

The following practices help us to live a life of love with the Sacred Heart:

1. **Morning Offering** (page 83) – daily offering our prayers, works, joys and sufferings to Christ;

2. **Daily Prayer to the Sacred Heart** (page 84) – daily renewing our pledge of love and loyalty to Christ the King;

3. **Holy Rosary** (page 86) – daily praying at least one decade, expressing devotion to our Blessed Mother, who unites our prayers to hers, and whose intercession thereby renders our prayers more effective;

4. **Conversation with Our Lord** – turning frequently to the Sacred Heart in prayer, speaking with Him throughout each day and offering such aspirations as *Sacred Heart of Jesus, have mercy on me; Heart of Jesus, help me to love You more and more;*

5. **Reading of the Gospels** – daily meditation on the Gospels whereby we become immersed in the life of Christ and come to know His love for us;

6. **Acts of Reparation** – making acts of love in reparation to the Sacred Heart of Jesus for injuries done to Him by the sins of mankind. (Reparation is necessary to satisfy divine justice. The foremost act of reparation, the only perfect one, is the Holy Sacrifice of the Mass. Other forms of reparation include making Holy Hours and offering our daily trials and sufferings in a spirit of penance and sacrifice to Our Lord.)

7. **Holy Sacrifice of the Mass** – frequent, even daily, participation when possible by at least one member of the family, particularly on the First Friday of every month, in accord with Our Lord's twelfth promise to Saint Margaret Mary Alacoque (page 10);

8. **Regular Holy Hours** – visiting the Blessed Sacrament for adoration in order to develop a great love for and devotion to the Real Presence of Jesus in the Holy Eucharist. If possible, making a Holy Hour at home or in a church on the Thursday night before First Friday in reparation to Our Lord according to His instruction to Saint Margaret Mary Alacoque: "'it was My will to suffer in the Garden of Olives…. To join with Me in this humble prayer which I then offered to My Father, you shall rise between eleven o'clock and midnight; you shall prostrate yourself with Me for *one hour…* both to appease the anger of God by imploring mercy for sinners, and to sweeten in some way the bitterness I felt when My Apostles abandoned Me, being unable to watch one hour with Me.' The generous sacrifice of an hour of one's sleep is richly rewarded, not only by remarkable conversions, especially in one's own family, but also by an increase of love for the Sacred Heart of Jesus" (*Enthronement of the Sacred Heart*, p. 37). Father Crawley-Boevey provides meditations for these Holy Hours in his book, *Holy Hours.*

9. **First Fridays and the Feast of the Sacred Heart** (which falls on the Friday after the Solemnity of Corpus Christi) – making it a family tradition to attend Holy Mass, and praying the *Act of Consecration* (page 40) or the *Act of Renewal* (page 85) in reparation for the lack of love for Christ in the Holy Eucharist;

10. **Promotion of the Enthronement and Consecration** – making the Sacred Heart of Jesus better known and loved, most especially by the loving witness of our lives.

CHAPTER 2

Preparation FOR THE Enthronement

The Necessity of Preparation

Anytime we are about to undertake an important action, we give ourselves ample time to prepare. Certainly, when we desire to consecrate ourselves to Christ, we want to prepare well. It would be a mockery of the worst sort to enthrone the image of the Sacred Heart of Jesus thoughtlessly, without regard for the profound meaning of our action. It would be a demonstration of the lack of reverence and the coldness toward Our Lord to which He referred in His fourth apparition to Saint Margaret Mary (page 5).

Since the Enthronement is a way of life for us, demanding our daily conversion of heart, we do not undertake it without considering carefully what it means for us. Our preparation should deepen in us our understanding and our desire for the Enthronement and Consecration.

The preparation has three principal parts: study, prayer and practical arrangements. Each part is important to the proper disposition of those involved. The goal of the preparation is hearts aflame with love for Christ. Only careful preparation and a thoughtful Act of Enthronement and Consecration will dispose minds and hearts to follow Christ the King, to trust in His never-failing love and to place our hearts into His.

Preparing by Study

The first important means of preparation is study. Study deepens our knowledge of the Enthronement and its meaning for our daily living. Father Mateo Crawley-Boevey has provided a complete presentation on the Enthronement and Consecration in his book, *Jesus King of Love*. Father Francis Larkin has also written an excellent book on the various aspects of the Enthronement entitled *Enthronement of the Sacred Heart*. Both books are highly recommended.

Preparing by Prayer

Before the image of the Sacred Heart is enthroned in a special place, we should prepare ourselves spiritually; consequently, the second means of preparation is prayer. Father Crawley-Boevey has suggested special prayers on each of the three days which immediately precede the day of Enthronement. This three-day period of prayer, called a *triduum*, can easily be adapted for use by any group and may include other special prayers and acts of charity.

Each day of the *Triduum of Prayers* includes a meditation on a mystery of Jesus' life as presented in Sacred Scripture, one decade of the Rosary, the *Litany of the Sacred Heart* and prayers to help prepare us for the outpouring of grace we will receive by consecrating ourselves to the Heart of Jesus.

Participation in the Holy Sacrifice of the Mass and reception of Holy Communion on each day of the triduum is highly recommended and is particularly fitting for all involved on the day of Enthronement.

The *Triduum of Prayers* begins on page 21 for Enthronement in the home, and on page 47 for Enthronement in other settings.

Practical Arrangements for Enthronement of the Sacred Heart

The place of the Enthronement (whether in the home, parish, school or other setting) must be fitting. In other words, it should be a central place, a place in which family or members of the community spend time each day. The living room, for example, is often the best place for the Enthronement in the home.

The image of the Sacred Heart may be enthroned on a small table upon which flowers, candles, a Bible, prayer intentions and pictures of absent loved ones or those in need of prayer can be placed. If the image is hung on a wall, a small shelf should be placed under it for the same objects. In any case, the place of Enthronement should reflect the great reverence and love which we have for Our Lord. It should be the most dignified and beautiful place in the room.

On the day of Enthronement, a separate table for the image and holy water should be set in a different room, or at least a different part of the room. The image will be carried from this table to its place of permanent Enthronement.

The Enthronement is fittingly led by a priest, if possible, but can also be led by a deacon, the head of the household, principal of the Catholic school, or other appropriate figure of authority.

Invite family and friends to the Rite of Enthronement. The invitation gives a strong witness to the Catholic faith and its practice, and has the potential of inspiring others to learn about the Enthronement, and eventually to enthrone the image of the Sacred Heart of Jesus in their own homes. Copies of the Enthronement Ceremony should be available for all who are invited so that they may participate as fully as possible.

Finally, it would be good to have some refreshments after the Enthronement so that all present can continue to express their joy on this grace-filled day of Enthronement and Consecration. The social time provides an excellent opportunity to explain to others the beauty of the Enthronement. It is a natural time to give witness to our love of the Sacred Heart of Jesus.

List of supplies:
Image of the Sacred Heart of Jesus
Holy Water
Bible
Candles
Copies of the Enthronement Ceremony

CHAPTER 3

Triduum of Prayers
FOR THE
Enthronement in the Home

THE FIRST DAY

To the Heart of Our King, Jesus of Bethlehem

SIGN OF THE CROSS

Leader: In the name of the Father, and of the Son, and of the Holy Spirit.

R/. **Amen.**

SCRIPTURE READING

Leader: The Third Joyful Mystery, *The Birth of Jesus in the Stable at Bethlehem*. This mystery centers on the truth of the Incarnation and our response of worship before Our Lord, Who is indeed God made man. In this mystery, we reflect on

Jesus being adored as King by His Mother Mary, His guardian Joseph, the shepherds and the Three Kings. In this mystery, we find the inspiration for our desire to enthrone the image of the Incarnate Redeemer, and for our constant adoration of Him.

Someone other than the leader reads:

A reading from the Holy Gospel according to Luke.

In those days a decree went out from Caesar Augustus that all the world should be enrolled. This was the first enrollment, when Quirinius was governor of Syria. And all went to be enrolled, each to his own city. And Joseph also went up from Galilee, from the city of Nazareth, to Judea, to the city of David, which is called Bethlehem, because he was of the house and lineage of David, to be enrolled with Mary his betrothed, who was with child.

And while they were there, the time came for her to be delivered. And she gave birth to her first-born son and wrapped him in swaddling cloths, and laid him in a manger, because there was no place for them in the inn. And in that region there were shepherds out in the field, keeping watch over their flock by night. And an angel of the Lord appeared to them, and the glory of the Lord shone around them, and they were filled with fear. And the angel said to them, "Be not afraid; for behold, I bring you good news of a great joy which will come to all the people; for to you is born this day in the city of David a Savior, who is Christ the Lord. And this will be a sign for you: you will find a baby wrapped in swaddling clothes and lying in a manger." And suddenly there was with the angel a multitude of the heavenly host praising God and saying, "Glory to God in the highest, and on earth peace among men with whom he is pleased."

When the angels went away from them into heaven, the shepherds said to one another, "Let us go over to Bethlehem and see this thing that has happened, which the Lord has made known to us." And they went with haste, and found Mary and Joseph, and the baby lying in a manger. And when they saw it they made known the saying which had been told them concerning this child; and all who heard it wondered at what the shepherds told them. But Mary kept all these things, pondering them in her heart. And the shepherds returned, glorifying and praising God for all they had heard and seen, as it had been told them. (*Luke* 2:1-20)

The Word of the Lord.
R/. **Thanks be to God.**

THE THIRD JOYFUL MYSTERY
The Birth of Our Lord
(1 *Our Father*, 10 *Hail Marys*, 1 *Glory Be*)

LITANY OF THE SACRED HEART
(See Appendix, page 87 or 92)

PRAYER
Leader: Let us pray. Sacred Heart of Jesus, we salute You, for You are the King of Kings, the Ruler of families and nations. But, sad to say, in many nations You have been dethroned and Your rights rejected. This is mainly because You were first dethroned in many families of which nations are composed.

Loving Master, we want to make up for this insult to Your Divine Majesty by lovingly enthroning You as King of our family. Like Mary and Joseph, like the shepherds and the Three Kings, we want to give You a royal welcome as they did when they adored You in Your humble home at Bethlehem.

Like them, we have no royal throne to offer You, but we can and we will offer something even more pleasing to You. In our home, Your throne will be a living throne, the loyal hearts of the members of this family; Your royal crown, our acts of love. O Mary, Queen of our home, by your loving submission to the will of God in all things, obtain for us the grace never to sadden the Heart of our King by willful disobedience to His Commandments or to those of His Church. May it be said of each of us what the Gospel says of Jesus, "He was obedient to them."

Good Saint Joseph, guardian of our family, help us to make our Enthronement the beginning of a new life of love in our home. Through the presence of the Sacred Heart of Jesus in our family circle, and through your powerful intercession, may we receive the grace to know our King more personally, love Him more ardently, and thus serve Him more faithfully. Amen.

INDULGENCED PRAYER

All: O Christ Jesus, I acknowledge You to be King of the universe; all that has been made is created by You. Exercise over me all Your sovereign rights. I hereby renew the promises of my Baptism, renouncing Satan and all his pomps and works, and I engage myself to lead henceforth a truly Christian life. And in a special manner do I undertake to bring about the triumph of the rights of God and His Church, so far as in me lies. Divine Heart of Jesus, I offer You my poor actions to obtain the acknowledgment by every heart of Your sacred kingly power. In such wisdom may the kingdom of Your peace be firmly established throughout all the earth.

Leader: Most Sacred Heart of Jesus,
R/. **Thy Kingdom come through Mary.**

Leader: Sacred Heart of Jesus,
R/. **protect our families.**

Leader: Immaculate Heart of Mary,
Queen of Heaven and of our home,
R/. **pray for us.**

Leader: Saint Joseph, friend of the Sacred Heart,
R/. **pray for us.**

Leader: Saint Michael, first champion of
the Kingship of Christ,
R/. **pray for us.**

Leader: Guardian Angels of our family,
R/. **pray for us.**

HYMN
Immaculate Mary (see Appendix, page 91)

THE SECOND DAY

To the Heart of Our Brother, Jesus of Nazareth

SIGN OF THE CROSS
Leader: In the name of the Father, and of the Son, and of the Holy Spirit.
R/. **Amen.**

SCRIPTURE READING
Leader: The Fifth Joyful Mystery, *The Finding of the Child Jesus in the Temple, and His Return to Nazareth.* This mystery inspires us to model the life of our family upon the Holy Family as we think of Jesus, the Son of God, living an ordinary life in the little home at Nazareth with Mary and Joseph. The care of Mary and Joseph for Jesus and His obedience to them are models for our relationships within the family as well as with others.

Someone other than the leader reads:
A reading from the Holy Gospel according to Luke.

And the child grew and became strong, filled with wisdom; and the favor of God was upon him. Now his parents went to Jerusalem every year at the feast of the Passover. And when he was twelve years old, they went up according to custom; and when the feast was ended, as they were returning, the boy Jesus stayed behind in Jerusalem. His parents did not know it, but supposing him to be in the company they went a day's journey, and they sought him among their kinsfolk and acquaintances; and when they did not find him, they returned to Jerusalem, seeking him.

After three days they found him in the temple, sitting among the teachers, listening to them and asking them questions; and all who heard him were amazed at his understanding and his answers. And when they saw him they were astonished; and his mother said to him, "Son, why have you treated us so? Behold, your father and I have been looking for you anxiously." And he said to them, "How is it that you sought me? Did you not know that I must be in my Father's house?" And they did not understand the saying which he spoke to them. And he went down with them and came to Nazareth, and was obedient to them; and his mother kept all these things in her heart. And Jesus increased in wisdom and in stature, and in favor with God and man. (*Luke* 2:40-52)

The Word of the Lord.
R/. **Thanks be to God.**

THE FIFTH JOYFUL MYSTERY
The Finding of the Child Jesus in the Temple
(1 *Our Father*, 10 *Hail Marys*, 1 *Glory Be*)

LITANY OF THE SACRED HEART
(See Appendix, page 87 or 92)

PRAYER
Leader: Let us pray. Dear Jesus, Son of God, when we call You "Brother," we speak the truth, for You are indeed just that. Saint John told us so when in his Gospel he wrote: "But to as many as received Him, He gave the power of becoming sons of God." Therefore we are Your adopted brothers and sisters and co-heirs of Heaven. But since You are a King, we too, have the privilege of being members of a royal family, as were Mary and Joseph.

How honored will we be to have our Brother-King come to dwell in our humble home in order to share our joys and sorrows! Once You are enthroned in our family, we will understand as never before the meaning of these words, "And the Word was made flesh and dwelt among us." No longer need we envy Mary and Joseph at Nazareth, for Your abiding presence in our home will make our family another Nazareth wherein we will vie with one another in giving You proofs of our love. We will do this especially by the practice of family charity, trying to love each other as You have loved us.

O Mary, Queen of Nazareth, Mother of Jesus, obtain for us the grace to appreciate the presence of your Divine Son enthroned in our home. Grant us a greater love for Jesus ever present in the Blessed Sacrament, a deeper love for Holy Mass, a more ardent longing to unite ourselves as often as possible with our loving Savior in Holy Communion.

Good Saint Joseph, you were privileged to share the joys and sorrows of your foster-Son at Nazareth. Teach us how to share our everyday joys and sorrows with our Brother Jesus here on earth, so that one day our entire family may join Mary and you in sharing the joys of Heaven, where we will see our King and Brother face to face and, with you, love, adore, thank and praise Him for all eternity. Amen.

INDULGENCED PRAYER

All: O Christ Jesus, I acknowledge You to be King of the universe; all that has been made is created by You. Exercise over me all Your sovereign rights. I hereby renew the promises of my Baptism, renouncing Satan and all his pomps and works, and I engage myself to lead henceforth a truly Christian life. And in a special manner do I undertake to bring about the triumph of the rights of God and His Church, so far as in me lies. Divine Heart of Jesus, I offer You my poor actions to obtain the acknowledgment by every heart of Your sacred kingly power. In such wisdom may the kingdom of Your peace be firmly established throughout all the earth.

Leader: Eucharistic Heart of Jesus,
R/. **Thy Kingdom come in our home.**

Leader: Our Lady of the Blessed Sacrament,
R/. **pray for us.**

Leader: Saint Joseph, foster-father of Our Lord
Jesus Christ and true spouse of Mary the Virgin,
R/. **pray for us.**

Leader: Saints Joachim and Anne,
parents of the Blessed Virgin Mary,
R/. **pray for us.**

Leader: Guardian Angels of our family,
R/. **pray for us.**

HYMN
To Jesus Christ, Our Sov'reign King (see Appendix, page 89)

THE THIRD DAY

To the Heart of Our Friend, Jesus of Bethany

SIGN OF THE CROSS

Leader: In the name of the Father, and of the Son, and of the Holy Spirit.

R/. **Amen.**

SCRIPTURE READING

Leader: The First Glorious Mystery, *The Resurrection*. Reflecting on this mystery helps us to recognize the living presence of Our Lord with us in the Church, and increases in us the desire to be with Him always. We think of Jesus rising in triumph from the tomb and hear Him promising Martha and Mary that their brother will rise again.

Someone other than the leader reads:

A reading from the Holy Gospel according to Luke.

Now a certain man was ill, Lazarus of Bethany, the village of Mary and her sister Martha. It was Mary who anointed the Lord with ointment and wiped his feet with her hair, whose brother Lazarus was ill. So the sisters sent to him, saying, "Lord, he whom you love is ill."

But when Jesus heard it he said, "This illness is not unto death; it is for the glory of God, so that the Son of God may be glorified by means of it." Now Jesus loved Martha and her sister and Lazarus. So when he heard that he was ill, he stayed two days longer in the place where he was. Then after this he said to the disciples, "Let us go into Judea again." The disciples said to him, "Rabbi, the Jews were but now seeking to stone you, and are you going there again?" Jesus answered, "Are there not twelve hours in the day? If any one walks in the day, he does not stumble, because he sees the light of this world. But if any one walks in the night, he stumbles, because the light is not in him." Thus he spoke, and then he said to them, "Our friend Lazarus has fallen asleep, but I go to awake him out of sleep." The disciples said to him, "Lord, if he has fallen asleep, he will recover." Now Jesus had spoken of his death, but they thought that he meant taking rest in sleep. Then Jesus told them plainly, "Lazarus is dead; and for your sake I am glad that I was not there, so that you may believe. But let us go to him." Thomas, called the Twin, said to his fellow disciples, "Let us also go, that we may die with him."

Now when Jesus came, he found that Lazarus had already been in the tomb four days. Bethany was near Jerusalem, about two miles off, and many of the Jews had come to Martha and Mary to console them concerning their brother. When Martha heard that Jesus was coming, she went and met him, while Mary sat in the house. Martha said to Jesus, "Lord, if you had been here, my brother would not have died. And even now I know that whatever you ask from God, God will give you." Jesus said to her, "Your brother will rise again." Martha said to him, "I know that he will rise again in the resurrection at the last day." Jesus said to her, "I am the resurrection and the life; he who believes in me, though he die, yet shall he live, and whoever lives and believes in me shall never die. Do you believe this?" She said to him, "Yes, Lord; I believe that you are the Christ, the Son of God, he who is coming into the world." (*John* 11:1-27)

The Word of the Lord.
R/. **Thanks be to God.**

THE FIRST GLORIOUS MYSTERY
The Resurrection of Jesus
(1 *Our Father*, 10 *Hail Marys*, 1 *Glory Be*)

LITANY OF THE SACRED HEART
(See Appendix, page 87 or 92)

PRAYER
Leader: Let us pray. "My delights are to be with the children of men." These words from the *Book of Proverbs* were certainly spoken about You, dear Jesus, Who came down to share our exile here below. You delight in being with us because we need You and You are our best Friend. You love all without exception: saints and sinners, the rich and the poor, the learned and the uneducated. You love all races and all peoples, but, above all, you love all families. You proved that love by spending thirty years in Your home at Nazareth, and during Your public life, many times You accepted invitations to visit families. You even told Zacchaeus the sinner, "I must stay in thy house today."

But there was one family for whom You had a special love, that of Lazarus, Martha and Mary. How many times did You not stay with that beloved family at Bethany! It was there You found rest and solace after the fatigue of Your labors and the insulting attacks of Your enemies. At Bethany, You were always received as a royal Guest, but also You were treated as a Brother and a Friend.

Dear Jesus, once You are enthroned in our home, we, too, want to be Your true friends. We want You to feel at home with us. We will try to console You for those who do not love You. We will serve You like Martha, listen to You like Mary, and thank

You as did Lazarus. We feel confident that You will richly bless our family as You did the family of Lazarus and all those families who invited You into their homes.

And if there are in our homes prodigal sons, lost sheep, sinners dead to the life of grace, we know that You will say to them as You did to Zacchaeus, "Today salvation has come to this house." You will be to them a loving Father, a Good Shepherd, a Divine Physician, for You are "the Resurrection and the Life."

O Mary, Mother of our best Friend, and Saint Joseph, our patron, obtain for us the grace to make our home a true Bethany of the Sacred Heart. May our friendship with Jesus be loving, loyal and lasting. May our daily living with our King and our Guest bring about a closer union of hearts, minds and wills so that our entire family, united with the Heart of Jesus here on earth, may remain united with Him and the Father and the Holy Spirit in our true home, Heaven, for all eternity! Amen.

INDULGENCED PRAYER

All: O Christ Jesus, I acknowledge You to be King of the universe; all that has been made is created by You. Exercise over me all Your sovereign rights. I hereby renew the promises of my Baptism, renouncing Satan and all his pomps and works, and I engage myself to lead henceforth a truly Christian life. And in a special manner do I undertake to bring about the triumph of the rights of God and His Church, so far as in me lies. Divine Heart of Jesus, I offer You my poor actions to obtain the acknowledgment by every heart of Your sacred kingly power. In such wisdom may the kingdom of Your peace be firmly established throughout all the earth.

Leader: Heart of Jesus, King, Brother and Friend
of our family, we welcome You to our home.
R/. **Thy Kingdom come.**

Leader: Our Lady of the Sacred Heart,
R/. **pray for us.**

Leader: Saint Joseph, model and
patron of lovers of the Sacred Heart,
R/. **pray for us.**

Leader: Saints Lazarus, Martha and Mary,
R/. **pray for us.**

Leader: Guardian Angels of our family,
R/. **pray for us.**

Leader: O Jesus, Friend of little children,
R/. **bless the little children of the whole world.**

HYMN
Holy God We Praise Thy Name (see Appendix, page 90)

34

CHAPTER 4

CEREMONY FOR THE ENTHRONEMENT
OF THE
Sacred Heart
IN THE HOME

After all the arrangements have been made, the Enthronement Ceremony begins at a table on which the image of the Sacred Heart and holy water have been placed. This table should be somewhat distant from the place of Enthronement in order to form a procession to the place of Enthronement. The priest will bless the image during the Enthronement Ceremony, but if a priest is not present, the image should be blessed beforehand, and the head of the house assumes the role of leader.

OPENING HYMN
To Jesus Christ, Our Sov'reign King (see Appendix, page 89)

SIGN OF THE CROSS
Leader: In the name of the Father, and of the Son, and of the Holy Spirit.
R/. **Amen.**

Leader: The Lord be with you.
R/. **And with your spirit.**

INTRODUCTION

Leader: "God is Love" (1 *John* 4:16), and all of His works serve to show this divine love to mankind. The writings of the Old Testament reveal that God's love created us in His image and likeness; it established a covenant with Abraham; it rescued the Chosen People from slavery in Egypt and brought them to the Promised Land. The fullest expression of God's love is the Person of Jesus Christ: "For God so loved the world that he gave his only-begotten Son, that whoever believes in him should not perish but have eternal life" (*John* 3:16). The Heart of Jesus Itself, in love with and wounded for mankind, is the most perfect symbol of the love of God. For this reason, "The prayer of the Church venerates and honors the *Heart of Jesus*.... It adores the incarnate Word and his Heart which, out of love for men, he allowed to be pierced by our sins" (*Catechism of the Catholic Church*, n. 2669).

The Enthronement of the Sacred Heart of Jesus, for which we are gathered, is an expression of our own love of God and the love which He shows to us. The enthroned image of the Sacred Heart expresses the true Kingship of Christ Who rules over us by giving up His life for us. It daily reminds each member of the family to follow in Christ's royal way by making reparation for sins and striving to serve God and neighbor more lovingly.

The image of the Sacred Heart of Jesus is enthroned to signify that Christ is He Who gives inspiration and direction to each member of the family. The Enthronement is a single act, but it represents a way of life by which each member of the family is transformed in Christ each day.

May the Enthronement truly be for this family a source of new vigor in living the Christian vocation, the vocation to love.

APOSTLES' CREED

Leader: As an act of loving faith in all of Jesus' teachings, and as an act of atonement for those who reject them or do not practice them, let us recite the Apostles' Creed together.

I believe in God, the Father Almighty,
Creator of Heaven and earth;
and in Jesus Christ, His only Son, Our Lord;
Who was conceived by the Holy Spirit,
born of the Virgin Mary,
suffered under Pontius Pilate, was crucified, died, and
    was buried.
He descended into Hell;
the third day He arose again from the dead.
He ascended into Heaven, and sits at the right hand of God,
    the Father Almighty;
from thence He shall come to judge the living and the dead.

I believe in the Holy Spirit,
the Holy Catholic Church,
the Communion of Saints,
the forgiveness of sins,
the resurrection of the body and life everlasting.
Amen.

SCRIPTURE READING
Someone other than the leader reads:
A reading from the First Letter of John.

Beloved, let us love one another; for love is of God, and he who loves is born of God and knows God. He who does not love does not know God; for God is love. In this the love of God was made manifest among us, that God sent his only-begotten Son into the world, so that we might live through him. In this is love, not that we loved God but that he loved us and sent his Son to be the expiation for our sins.

Beloved, if God so loved us, we also ought to love one another. No man has ever seen God; if we love one another, God abides in us and his love is perfected in us. By this we know that we abide in him and he in us, because he has given us of his own Spirit. And we have seen and testify that the Father has sent his Son as the Savior of the world. Whoever confesses that Jesus is the Son of God, God abides in him, and he in God. So we know and believe the love God has for us. (1 *John* 4:7-16a)

The Word of the Lord.
R/. Thanks be to God.

Other readings may be used, particularly the account of the Annunciation (*Luke* 1:26-33), Our Lord's meeting with Zacchaeus (*Luke* 19:1-10) or Our Lord's visit to the home of Martha and Mary (*Luke* 10:38-42).

REFLECTION (optional)
A brief reflection may be offered by the leader.

BLESSING OF THE IMAGE

The image of the Sacred Heart is to be blessed by a priest. If an image of the Immaculate Heart of Mary is installed along with the Sacred Heart, the blessing found on page 81 may be used. If the images were previously blessed, the blessings are omitted at this time.

Priest:
Lord,
although Your glory lies beyond our sight,
out of Your great love
You have revealed Yourself in the Heart of Christ.
Bless ✠ this image of Your Son.
May those who venerate it
honor Christ by growing in His likeness,
Who is Lord for ever and ever.
R/. **Amen.**

The priest sprinkles the image with holy water.

ACT OF ENTHRONEMENT

For the procession, the head of the household carries the image of the Sacred Heart, another family member carries the Bible, and others may carry candles. The head of the household, accompanied by the priest, members of the household, and guests then processes with the image to the place of Enthronement. The head of the household enthrones the image of the Sacred Heart in the selected place saying:

I now enthrone Jesus as King and Friend of our family.

The person carrying the Bible then places it near the image of the Sacred Heart and says:

We are nourished by the Body and Blood of Christ, and by the Word of God.

The candles are then placed on either side of the image as the candle bearers (or all present, if there are no candle bearers) say the following together:

The Lord sits enthroned as King forever! (*Psalm* 29:10b) **All that the Lord has spoken we will do, and we will be obedient.** (*Exodus* 24:7)

ACT OF CONSECRATION OF THE FAMILY

All kneel and say in unison:

O Sacred Heart of Jesus, Who made known to Saint Margaret Mary Your great desire to reign over Christian families, we are gathered here today to proclaim Your complete rule over our family. From now on we promise to lead a Christ-like life; we will strive to develop in our home all the virtues which bring with them the peace that You promised. And we will not compromise with the spirit of secularism which You have so strongly denounced.

You will rule over our minds through our deep and living faith. You will be King of our hearts by our generous love for You; and we will cultivate this love by the frequent reception of You in Holy Communion.

Divine Heart of Jesus, preside over our family gatherings; bless all our family undertakings, both spiritual and temporal. Sanctify our joys and comfort us in our sorrows. And if any member of our family should have the misfortune to offend You seriously, remind him, O Sacred Heart of Jesus, of Your infinite love and mercy for the penitent sinner.

And when the hour of separation comes, when death brings its sorrows into our family, whether we go or whether we stay, we will humbly accept Your Divine Will. And at the same time we will console and comfort ourselves with the thought that the time will come when our whole family will be united lovingly with You in Heaven forever. There we shall sing a hymn of praise to the infinite mercy and love of Your Sacred Heart.

We ask the Immaculate Heart of Mary and our glorious protector, Saint Joseph, to offer You this family Consecration.

May the memory of this Consecration be with us always.

Glory to the Divine Heart of Jesus, our King!

Praise to the Divine Heart of Jesus that brought us salvation. To It be honor and glory forever.

Amen.

If an image of the Immaculate Heart of Mary is installed, the *Act of Consecration to the Immaculate Heart* found on page 82 is made at this point.

INTERCESSIONS

Leader: Lord Jesus, You told us that "whatever you ask the Father in my name, he will give to you." In Your name, and with great confidence in Your love, we now offer these prayers:

Someone other than the leader proposes the intercessions:
For the grace of being faithful to this covenant with Jesus and our renewed way of life in Him, let us pray:
R/. **Lord, hear our prayer.**

For an increase of personal, generous love for Jesus, and a greater trust in His merciful love, let us pray:
R/. **Lord, hear our prayer.**

That the Holy Spirit may always find our hearts responsive to His call, let us pray:
R/. **Lord, hear our prayer.**

For a deeper appreciation of the greatest gift of the Heart of Jesus, the Holy Eucharist, through frequent participation in the Holy Sacrifice of the Mass and Holy Communion, especially on First Fridays, let us pray:
R/. **Lord, hear our prayer.**

That we may desire to receive the Sacrament of Confession more often in order to increase our love for Jesus and to avoid sin, let us pray:
R/. **Lord, hear our prayer.**

That our family members who are absent may be protected
in all they do, and that all our beloved family who have
died may be united to the Heart of Jesus in Heaven
for ever, let us pray:
R/. **Lord, hear our prayer.**

Leader:
God our Father,
through the Sacred Heart of Your Son, Jesus,
You pour forth Your eternal love upon us.
By the Enthronement of the image of Jesus' Heart
and our Consecration to It,
may we show our love to You and to the world.
We ask this through the same Christ Our Lord.
R/. **Amen.**

Leader: Let us conclude by calling on the Mother of God, Mary Most Holy:

HAIL HOLY QUEEN

All: **Hail, Holy Queen, Mother of Mercy, our life, our sweetness, and our hope! To thee do we cry, poor banished children of Eve; to thee do we send up our sighs, mourning and weeping in this valley of tears. Turn then, most gracious advocate, thine eyes of mercy toward us, and after this our exile, show unto us the blessed fruit of thy womb, Jesus. O clement, O loving, O sweet Virgin Mary.**

Leader: Pray for us, O holy Mother of God.
R/. **That we may be made worthy of the promises of Christ.**

Leader: Most Sacred Heart of Jesus,
R/. **have mercy on us.**

Leader: Immaculate Heart of Mary,
R/. **pray for us!**

Leader: Saint Joseph,
R/. **pray for us!**

Leader: Our Guardian Angels,
R/. **pray for us!**

Leader: Most Sacred Heart of Jesus,
R/. **have mercy on us.**

CLOSING PRAYER

Leader: Let us pray. O Father of mercies and God of all consolation, Who by the exceeding love with which You have loved us, have given us the Heart of Your beloved Son so that having but one heart with Him, we may love You perfectly, grant, we beseech You, that our hearts, being consumed in unity with the Heart of Jesus and with one another, may perform all our works in accord with His humility and charity and that, by His mediation, the just desires of our hearts may be accomplished, through the same Christ Our Lord.
R/. **Amen.**

If a priest is present, the Rite of Enthronement concludes with a blessing. Otherwise, the Rite concludes with the *Sign of the Cross.*

BLESSING AND DISMISSAL

Priest: The Lord be with you.
R/. **And with your spirit.**

Priest: May almighty God bless you,
the Father, the Son, and ✠ the Holy Spirit.
R/. **Amen.**

Priest: Go in peace.
R/. **Thanks be to God.**

CLOSING HYMN

Holy God We Praise Thy Name (see Appendix, page 90)

The Certificate of Enthronement found on page 97 may be signed at this time.

CHAPTER 5

Triduum of Prayers
FOR THE ENTHRONEMENT IN
*Parishes, Catholic Schools
and Other Settings*

THE FIRST DAY

To the Heart of Our King, Jesus of Bethlehem

SIGN OF THE CROSS
Leader: In the name of the Father, and of the Son, and of the Holy Spirit.
R/. Amen.

SCRIPTURE READING
Leader: The Third Joyful Mystery, *The Birth of Jesus in the Stable at Bethlehem*. This mystery centers on the truth of the

Incarnation, and our response of worship before Our Lord, Who is indeed God made man. In this mystery, we reflect on Jesus being adored as King by His Mother Mary, His guardian Joseph, the shepherds and the Three Kings. In this mystery, we find the inspiration for our desire to enthrone the image of the Incarnate Redeemer, and for our constant adoration of Him.

Someone other than the leader reads:

A reading from the Holy Gospel according to Luke.

In those days a decree went out from Caesar Augustus that all the world should be enrolled. This was the first enrollment, when Quirinius was governor of Syria. And all went to be enrolled, each to his own city. And Joseph also went up from Galilee, from the city of Nazareth, to Judea, to the city of David, which is called Bethlehem, because he was of the house and lineage of David, to be enrolled with Mary his betrothed, who was with child.

And while they were there, the time came for her to be delivered. And she gave birth to her first-born son and wrapped him in swaddling cloths, and laid him in a manger, because there was no place for them in the inn. And in that region there were shepherds out in the field, keeping watch over their flock by night. And an angel of the Lord appeared to them, and the glory of the Lord shone around them, and they were filled with fear. And the angel said to them, "Be not afraid; for behold, I bring you good news of a great joy which will come to all the people; for to you is born this day in the city of David a Savior, who is Christ the Lord. And this will be a sign for you: you will find a baby wrapped in swaddling clothes and lying in a manger." And suddenly there was with the angel a multitude of the heavenly host praising God and saying, "Glory to God in the highest, and on earth peace among men with whom he is pleased."

When the angels went away from them into heaven, the shepherds said to one another, "Let us go over to Bethlehem and see this thing that has happened, which the Lord has made known to us." And they went with haste, and found Mary and Joseph, and the baby lying in a manger. And when they saw it they made known the saying which had been told them concerning this child; and all who heard it wondered at what the shepherds told them. But Mary kept all these things, pondering them in her heart. And the shepherds returned, glorifying and praising God for all they had heard and seen, as it had been told them. (*Luke* 2:1-20)

The Word of the Lord.
R/. **Thanks be to God.**

THE THIRD JOYFUL MYSTERY
The Birth of Our Lord
(1 *Our Father*, 10 *Hail Marys*, 1 *Glory Be*)

LITANY OF THE SACRED HEART
(See Appendix, page 87 or 92)

PRAYER
Leader: Let us pray. Sacred Heart of Jesus, we salute You, for You are the King of Kings, the Ruler of families and nations. But, sad to say, in many nations You have been dethroned and Your rights rejected. This is mainly because You were first dethroned in many families of which nations are composed.

Loving Master, we want to make up for this insult to Your Divine Majesty by lovingly enthroning You as our King. Like Mary and Joseph, like the shepherds and the Three Kings, we want to give You a royal welcome as they did when they adored You in Your humble home at Bethlehem.

Like them, we have no royal throne to offer You, but we can and we will offer something even more pleasing to You. Your throne will be a living throne, our loyal hearts; your royal crown, our acts of love. O Mary, our Queen, by your loving submission to the will of God in all things, obtain for us the grace never to sadden the Heart of our King by willful disobedience to His Commandments or to those of His Church. May it be said of each of us what the Gospel says of Jesus, "He was obedient to them."

Good Saint Joseph, our guardian, help us to make our Enthronement the beginning of a new life of love for us. Through the presence of the Sacred Heart of Jesus, and through your powerful intercession, may we receive the grace to know our King more personally, love Him more ardently, and thus serve Him more faithfully. Amen.

INDULGENCED PRAYER

All: O Christ Jesus, I acknowledge You to be King of the universe; all that has been made is created by You. Exercise over me all Your sovereign rights. I hereby renew the promises of my Baptism, renouncing Satan and all his pomps and works, and I engage myself to lead henceforth a truly Christian life. And in a special manner do I undertake to bring about the triumph of the rights of God and His Church, so far as in me lies. Divine Heart of Jesus, I offer You my poor actions to obtain the acknowledgment by every heart of Your sacred kingly power. In such wisdom may the kingdom of Your peace be firmly established throughout all the earth.

Leader: Most Sacred Heart of Jesus,
R/. **Thy Kingdom come through Mary.**

Leader: Sacred Heart of Jesus,
R/. **protect us.**

Leader: Immaculate Heart of Mary, Queen of Heaven,
R/. **pray for us.**

Leader: Saint Joseph, friend of the Sacred Heart,
R/. **pray for us.**

Leader: Saint Michael, first champion of the Kingship of Christ,
R/. **pray for us.**

Leader: Guardian Angels,
R/. **pray for us.**

HYMN
Immaculate Mary (see Appendix, page 91)

THE SECOND DAY

To the Heart of Our Brother, Jesus of Nazareth

SIGN OF THE CROSS

Leader: In the name of the Father, and of the Son, and of the Holy Spirit.

R/. **Amen.**

SCRIPTURE READING

Leader: The Fifth Joyful Mystery, *The Finding of the Child Jesus in the Temple, and His Return to Nazareth.* This mystery inspires us to model our lives upon the Holy Family as we think of Jesus, the Son of God, living an ordinary life in the little home at Nazareth with Mary and Joseph. The care of Mary and Joseph for Jesus and His obedience to them are models for our relationships within the family as well as with others.

Someone other than the leader reads:

A reading from the Holy Gospel according to Luke.

And the child grew and became strong, filled with wisdom; and the favor of God was upon him. Now his parents went to Jerusalem every year at the feast of the Passover. And when he was twelve years old, they went up according to custom; and when the feast was ended, as they were returning, the boy Jesus stayed behind in Jerusalem. His parents did not know it, but supposing him to be in the company they went a day's journey, and they sought him among their kinsfolk and acquaintances; and when they did not find him, they returned to Jerusalem, seeking him.

After three days they found him in the temple, sitting among the teachers, listening to them and asking them questions; and all who heard him were amazed at his understanding and his answers. And when they saw him they were astonished; and his mother said to him, "Son, why have you treated us so? Behold, your father and I have been looking for you anxiously." And he said to them, "How is it that you sought me? Did you not know that I must be in my Father's house?" And they did not understand the saying which he spoke to them. And he went down with them and came to Nazareth, and was obedient to them; and his mother kept all these things in her heart. And Jesus increased in wisdom and in stature, and in favor with God and man. (*Luke* 2:40-52)

The Word of the Lord.
R/. **Thanks be to God.**

THE FIFTH JOYFUL MYSTERY
The Finding of the Child Jesus in the Temple
(1 *Our Father*, 10 *Hail Marys*, 1 *Glory Be*)

LITANY OF THE SACRED HEART
(See Appendix, page 87 or 92)

PRAYER
Leader: Let us pray. Dear Jesus, Son of God, when we call You "Brother," we speak the truth, for You are indeed just that. Saint John told us so when in his Gospel he wrote: "But to as many as received Him, He gave the power of becoming sons of God." Therefore we are Your adopted brothers and sisters and co-heirs of Heaven. But since You are a King, we too, have the privilege of being members of a royal family, as were Mary and Joseph.

How honored will we be to have our Brother-King come to dwell with us in order to share our joys and sorrows! Once You are enthroned, we will understand as never before the meaning of these words, "And the Word was made flesh and dwelt among us." No longer need we envy Mary and Joseph at Nazareth, for Your abiding presence will make us another Nazareth wherein we will vie with one another in giving You proofs of our love. We will do this especially by the practice of Christian charity, trying to love each other as You have loved us.

O Mary, Queen of Nazareth, Mother of Jesus, obtain for us the grace to appreciate the presence of your Divine Son Who is soon to be enthroned. Grant us a greater love for Jesus ever present in the Blessed Sacrament, a deeper love for Holy Mass, a more ardent longing to unite ourselves as often as possible with our loving Savior in Holy Communion.

Good Saint Joseph, you were privileged to share the joys and sorrows of your foster-Son at Nazareth. Teach us how to share our everyday joys and sorrows with our Brother Jesus here on earth, so that one day we may join you and Mary in sharing the joys of Heaven, where we will see our King and Brother face to face and, with you, love, adore, thank and praise Him for all eternity. Amen.

INDULGENCED PRAYER

All: O Christ Jesus, I acknowledge You to be King of the universe; all that has been made is created by You. Exercise over me all Your sovereign rights. I hereby renew the promises of my Baptism, renouncing Satan and all his pomps and works, and I engage myself to lead henceforth a truly Christian life. And in a special manner do I undertake to bring about the triumph of the rights of God and His Church, so far as in me lies. Divine Heart of Jesus, I offer You my poor actions to obtain the acknowledgment by every heart of Your sacred kingly power. In such wisdom may the kingdom of Your peace be firmly established throughout all the earth.

Leader: Eucharistic Heart of Jesus,
R/. Thy Kingdom come in our *(parish, school, or other setting).*

Leader: Our Lady of the Blessed Sacrament,
R/. pray for us.

Leader: Saint Joseph, foster-father of Our Lord
Jesus Christ and true spouse of Mary the Virgin,
R/. pray for us.

Leader: Saints Joachim and Anne,
parents of the Blessed Virgin Mary,
R/. pray for us.

Leader: Guardian Angels,
R/. pray for us.

HYMN

To Jesus Christ, Our Sov'reign King (see Appendix, page 89)

THE THIRD DAY

To the Heart of Our Friend, Jesus of Bethany

SIGN OF THE CROSS

Leader: In the name of the Father, and of the Son, and of the Holy Spirit.

R/. **Amen.**

SCRIPTURE READING

Leader: The First Glorious Mystery, *The Resurrection*. Reflecting on this mystery helps us to recognize the living presence of Our Lord with us in the Church, and increases in us the desire to be with Him always. We think of Jesus rising in triumph from the tomb and hear Him promising Martha and Mary that their brother will rise again.

Someone other than the leader reads:

A reading from the Holy Gospel according to John.

Now a certain man was ill, Lazarus of Bethany, the village of Mary and her sister Martha. It was Mary who anointed the Lord with ointment and wiped his feet with her hair, whose brother Lazarus was ill. So the sisters sent to him, saying, "Lord, he whom you love is ill."

But when Jesus heard it he said, "This illness is not unto death; it is for the glory of God, so that the Son of God may be glorified by means of it." Now Jesus loved Martha and her sister and Lazarus. So when he heard that he was ill, he stayed two days longer in the place where he was. Then after this he said to the disciples, "Let us go into Judea again." The disciples said to him, "Rabbi, the Jews were but now seeking to stone you, and are you going there again?" Jesus answered, "Are there not twelve hours in the day? If any one walks in the day, he does not stumble, because he sees the light of this world. But if any one walks in the night, he stumbles, because the light is not in him." Thus he spoke, and then he said to them, "Our friend Lazarus has fallen asleep, but I go to awake him out of sleep." The disciples said to him, "Lord, if he has fallen asleep, he will recover." Now Jesus had spoken of his death, but they thought that he meant taking rest in sleep. Then Jesus told them plainly, "Lazarus is dead; and for your sake I am glad that I was not there, so that you may believe. But let us go to him." Thomas, called the Twin, said to his fellow disciples, "Let us also go, that we may die with him."

Now when Jesus came, he found that Lazarus had already been in the tomb four days. Bethany was near Jerusalem, about two miles off, and many of the Jews had come to Martha and Mary to console them concerning their brother. When Martha heard that Jesus was coming, she went and met him, while Mary sat in the house. Martha said to Jesus, "Lord, if you had been here, my brother would not have died. And even now I know that whatever you ask from God, God will give you." Jesus said to her, "Your brother will rise again." Martha said to him, "I know that he will rise again in the resurrection at the last day." Jesus said to her, "I am the resurrection and the life; he who believes in me, though he die, yet shall he live, and whoever lives and believes in me shall never die. Do you believe this?" She said to him, "Yes, Lord; I believe that you are the Christ, the Son of God, he who is coming into the world." (*John* 11:1-27)

The Word of the Lord.
R/. **Thanks be to God.**

THE FIRST GLORIOUS MYSTERY
The Resurrection of Jesus
(1 *Our Father*, 10 *Hail Marys*, 1 *Glory Be*)

LITANY OF THE SACRED HEART
(See Appendix, page 87 or 92)

PRAYER
Leader: Let us pray. "My delights are to be with the children of men." These words from the *Book of Proverbs* were certainly spoken about You, dear Jesus, Who came down to share our exile here below. You delight in being with us because we need You and You are our best Friend. You love all without exception: saints and sinners, the rich and the poor, the learned and the uneducated. You love all races and all peoples, but, above all, you love all families. You proved that love by spending thirty years in Your home at Nazareth, and during Your public life, many times You accepted invitations to visit families. You even told Zacchaeus the sinner, "I must stay in thy house today."

But there was one family for whom You had a special love, that of Lazarus, Martha and Mary. How many times did You not stay with that beloved family at Bethany! It was there You found rest and solace after the fatigue of Your labors and the insulting attacks of Your enemies. At Bethany, You were always received as a royal Guest, but also You were treated as a Brother and a Friend.

Dear Jesus, once You are enthroned, we too, want to be Your true friends. We want You to feel at home with us. We will try to console You for those who do not love You. We will serve You like Martha, listen to You like Mary, and thank You as did Lazarus. We feel confident that You will richly bless us as You did the family of Lazarus and all those families who invited You into their homes.

And if there are in this place prodigal sons, lost sheep, sinners dead to the life of grace, we know that You will say to them as You did to Zacchaeus, "Today salvation has come to this house." You will be to them a loving Father, a Good Shepherd, a Divine Physician, for You are "the Resurrection and the Life."

O Mary, Mother of our best Friend, and Saint Joseph our patron, obtain for us the grace to make this place a true Bethany of the Sacred Heart. May our friendship with Jesus be loving, loyal and lasting. May our daily living with our King and our Guest bring about a closer union of hearts, minds and wills so that each of us, united with the Heart of Jesus here on earth, may remain united with Him and the Father and the Holy Spirit in our true home, Heaven, for all eternity! Amen.

INDULGENCED PRAYER

All: O Christ Jesus, I acknowledge You to be King of the universe; all that has been made is created by You. Exercise over me all Your sovereign rights. I hereby renew the promises of my Baptism, renouncing Satan and all his pomps and works, and I engage myself to lead henceforth a truly Christian life. And in a special manner do I undertake to bring about the triumph of the rights of God and His Church, so far as in me lies. Divine Heart of Jesus, I offer You my poor actions to obtain the acknowledgment by every heart of Your sacred kingly power. In such wisdom may the kingdom of Your peace be firmly established throughout all the earth.

Leader: Heart of Jesus, King, Brother
and Friend, we welcome You.
R/. **Thy Kingdom come.**

Leader: Our Lady of the Sacred Heart,
R/. **pray for us.**

Leader: Saint Joseph, model and
patron of lovers of the Sacred Heart,
R/. **pray for us.**

Leader: Saints Lazarus, Martha and Mary,
R/. **pray for us.**

Leader: Guardian Angels,
R/. **pray for us.**

Leader: O Jesus, Friend of little children,
R/. **bless the little children of the whole world.**

HYMN
Holy God We Praise Thy Name (see Appendix, page 90)

60

CHAPTER 6

CEREMONY FOR THE ENTHRONEMENT
OF THE

Sacred Heart

IN PARISHES, CATHOLIC SCHOOLS
AND OTHER SETTINGS

The Enthronement is fittingly carried out in parishes, Catholic schools and other settings where every activity is directed to the Christian growth of parishioners, students, families and other members of the faithful. The Enthronement publicly proclaims the rule of the Heart of Jesus over the persons and activities of the place. It is an act of reparation for the offenses committed against His Heart and, by the *Act of Consecration*, a pledge to honor the Sacred Heart now and in the future.

Ideally, the Enthronement takes place in the context of the Holy Sacrifice of the Mass. After suitable preparation, the Enthronement is carried out by a priest and his parishioners, by a school's administrators and its staff, students and guests, or by members of any other Catholic community or organization.

OPTION A

ENTHRONEMENT OUTSIDE OF HOLY MASS

The Enthronement Ceremony begins at a table on which the image of the Sacred Heart and holy water have been placed. This table should be somewhat distant from the place of Enthronement so that a procession may be formed to the place of Enthronement. The priest will bless the image during the Enthronement Ceremony, but if a priest is not present, the image should be blessed beforehand, and another figure of authority assumes the role of leader.

OPENING HYMN
To Jesus Christ, Our Sov'reign King (see Appendix, page 89)

SIGN OF THE CROSS
Leader: In the name of the Father, and of the Son, and of the Holy Spirit.
R/. **Amen.**

Leader: The Lord be with you.
R/. **And with your spirit.**

INTRODUCTION

Leader: "God is Love" (1 *John* 4:16), and all of His works serve to show this divine love to mankind. The writings of the Old Testament reveal that God's love created us in His image and likeness; it established a covenant with Abraham; it rescued the Chosen People from slavery in Egypt and brought them to the Promised Land. The fullest expression of God's love is the Person of Jesus Christ: "For God so loved the world that he gave his only-begotten Son, that whoever believes in him should not perish but have eternal life" (*John* 3:16). The Heart of Jesus Itself, in love with and wounded for mankind, is the most perfect symbol of the love of God. For this reason, "The prayer of the Church venerates and honors the *Heart of Jesus....* It adores the incarnate Word and his Heart which, out of love for men, he allowed to be pierced by our sins" (*Catechism of the Catholic Church*, n. 2669).

The Enthronement of the Sacred Heart of Jesus, for which we are gathered, is an expression of our own love of God and the love which He shows to us. The enthroned image of the Sacred Heart expresses the true Kingship of Christ Who rules over us by giving up His life for us. It daily reminds each of us to follow in Christ's royal way by making reparation for sins and striving to serve God and neighbor more lovingly.

The image of the Sacred Heart of Jesus is enthroned to signify that Christ is He Who gives inspiration and direction to each of us. The Enthronement is a single act, but it represents a way of life by which each of us is transformed in Christ each day.

May the Enthronement truly be for us a source of new vigor in living the Christian vocation, the vocation to love.

APOSTLES' CREED

Leader: As an act of loving faith in all of Jesus' teachings, and as an act of atonement for those who reject them or do not practice them, let us recite the Apostles' Creed together.

All: I believe in God, the Father Almighty,
Creator of Heaven and earth;
and in Jesus Christ, His only Son, Our Lord;
Who was conceived by the Holy Spirit,
born of the Virgin Mary,
suffered under Pontius Pilate, was crucified, died,
    and was buried.
He descended into Hell;
the third day He arose again from the dead.
He ascended into Heaven, and sits at the right hand of God,
    the Father Almighty;
from thence He shall come to judge the living and the dead.

I believe in the Holy Spirit,
the Holy Catholic Church,
the Communion of Saints,
the forgiveness of sins,
the resurrection of the body and life everlasting.
Amen.

SCRIPTURE READING

Someone other than the leader reads:

A reading from the First Letter of John.

Beloved, let us love one another; for love is of God, and he who loves is born of God and knows God. He who does not love does not know God; for God is love. In this the love of God was made manifest among us, that God sent his only-begotten Son into the world, so that we might live through him. In this is love, not that we loved God but that he loved us and sent his Son to be the expiation for our sins.

Beloved, if God so loved us, we also ought to love one another. No man has ever seen God; if we love one another, God abides in us and his love is perfected in us. By this we know that we abide in him and he in us, because he has given us of his own Spirit. And we have seen and testify that the Father has sent his Son as the Savior of the world. Whoever confesses that Jesus is the Son of God, God abides in him, and he in God. So we know and believe the love God has for us. (1 *John* 4:7-16a)

The Word of the Lord.
R/. **Thanks be to God.**

Other readings may be used, particularly the account of the Annunciation (*Luke* 1:26-33), Our Lord's meeting with Zacchaeus (*Luke* 19:1-10) or Our Lord's visit to the home of Martha and Mary (*Luke* 10:38-42).

REFLECTION (optional)
A brief reflection may be offered by the leader.

BLESSING OF THE IMAGE

The image of the Sacred Heart is to be blessed by a priest. If an image of the Immaculate Heart of Mary is installed, the blessing found on page 81 may be used. If the images were previously blessed, the blessings are omitted at this time.

Priest:

Lord,

although Your glory lies beyond our sight,

out of Your great love

You have revealed Yourself in the Heart of Christ.

Bless ✠ this image of Your Son.

May those who venerate it

honor Christ by growing in His likeness,

Who is Lord for ever and ever.

R/. **Amen.**

The priest sprinkles the image with holy water.

ACT OF ENTHRONEMENT

For the procession, an incense bearer, cross and candle bearers, the leader carrying the image of the Sacred Heart, and a person carrying the Bible are followed by the parishioners, school community, or other members of the faithful. All process to the place of Enthronement. A hymn may accompany the procession.

When all arrive at the place of Enthronement, the leader enthrones the image of the Sacred Heart in the selected place saying:

I now enthrone Jesus as King and Friend of our *(parish, school, or other setting).*

The person carrying the Bible then places it near the image of the Sacred Heart and says:

We are nourished by the Body and Blood of Christ, and by the Word of God.

The candles are then placed on either side of the image as the candle bearers say together:

The Lord sits enthroned as King forever! *(Psalm* 29:10b) **All that the Lord has spoken we will do, and we will be obedient.** *(Exodus* 24:7)

If incense is used, the image is incensed.

ACT OF CONSECRATION

If possible, all kneel and say in unison:

To the Sacred Heart of Our Lord, Jesus Christ, we give ourselves and consecrate our lives, our actions, pains, and sufferings, so that we may be unwilling to make use of any part of our being other than to honor, love, and glorify Your Sacred Heart.

This is our unchanging purpose, namely, to be all Yours and to do all things for the love of You, at the same time renouncing with all our hearts whatever is displeasing to You. We therefore take You, O Sacred Heart, to be the only object of our love, the guardian of our lives, our assurance of salvation, the remedy of our weakness, the atonement for all our faults, and our sure refuge at the hour of death.

Be then, O Heart of goodness, our justification before God the Father. O Heart of love, we put all our confidence in You, for we fear everything from our own weakness and frailty, but we hope for all things from Your goodness and bounty.

Remove from us all that can displease You or resist Your Holy Will; let Your pure love imprint Your image so deeply upon our hearts that we shall never be able to forget You or to be separated from You.

May we obtain from Your loving kindness the grace of having our names written in Your Heart, for in You we desire to place all our happiness and glory, living and dying in You, Who live and reign with the Father and the Holy Spirit, one God, for ever and ever. Amen.

If an image of the Immaculate Heart of Mary is installed, the *Act of Consecration to the Immaculate Heart* found on page 82 is made at this point.

INTERCESSIONS

Leader: Lord Jesus, You told us that "whatever you ask the Father in my name, he will give to you." In Your name, and with great confidence in Your love, we now offer these prayers:

Someone other than the leader proposes the intercessions:
For the grace of being faithful to this covenant with Jesus and our renewed way of life in Him, let us pray:
R/. **Lord, hear our prayer.**

For an increase of personal, generous love for Jesus, and a greater trust in His merciful love, let us pray:
R/. **Lord, hear our prayer.**

That the Holy Spirit may always find our hearts responsive to His call, let us pray:
R/. **Lord, hear our prayer.**

For a deeper appreciation of the greatest gift of the Heart of Jesus, the Holy Eucharist, through frequent participation in the Holy Sacrifice of the Mass and Holy Communion, especially on First Fridays, let us pray:
R/. **Lord, hear our prayer.**

That we may desire to receive the Sacrament of Confession more often in order to increase our love for Jesus and to avoid sin, let us pray:
R/. **Lord, hear our prayer.**

That those who are absent may be protected in all they do,
and that all our beloved who have died may be united to the
Heart of Jesus in Heaven for ever, let us pray:
R/. **Lord, hear our prayer.**

Leader:
God our Father,
through the Sacred Heart of Your Son, Jesus,
You pour forth Your eternal love upon us.
By the Enthronement of the image of Jesus' Heart
and our Consecration to It,
may we show our love to You and to the world.
We ask this through the same Christ Our Lord.
R/. **Amen.**

Leader: Let us conclude by calling on the Mother of God, Mary Most Holy:

HAIL HOLY QUEEN

All: **Hail, Holy Queen, Mother of Mercy, our life, our sweetness, and our hope! To thee do we cry, poor banished children of Eve; to thee do we send up our sighs, mourning and weeping in this valley of tears. Turn then, most gracious advocate, thine eyes of mercy toward us, and after this our exile, show unto us the blessed fruit of thy womb, Jesus. O clement, O loving, O sweet Virgin Mary.**

Leader: Pray for us, O holy Mother of God.
R/. **That we may be made worthy of the promises of Christ.**

Leader: Most Sacred Heart of Jesus,
R/. **have mercy on us.**

Leader: Immaculate Heart of Mary,
R/. **pray for us!**

Leader: Saint Joseph,
R/. **pray for us!**

Leader: Our Guardian Angels,
R/. **pray for us!**

Leader: Most Sacred Heart of Jesus,
R/. **have mercy on us.**

CLOSING PRAYER

Leader: Let us pray. O Father of mercies and God of all consolation, Who by the exceeding love with which You have loved us, have given us the Heart of Your beloved Son so that having but one heart with Him, we may love You perfectly, grant, we beseech You, that our hearts, being consumed in unity with the Heart of Jesus and with one another, may perform all our works in accord with His humility and charity and that, by His mediation, the just desires of our hearts may be accomplished, through the same Christ Our Lord.
R/. **Amen.**

If a priest is present, the Rite of Enthronement concludes with a blessing. Otherwise, the Rite concludes with the *Sign of the Cross.*

BLESSING AND DISMISSAL

Priest: The Lord be with you.
R/. **And with your spirit.**

Priest: May almighty God bless you,
the Father, the Son, and ✠ the Holy Spirit.
R/. **Amen.**

Priest: Go in peace.
R/. **Thanks be to God.**

CLOSING HYMN

Holy God We Praise Thy Name (see Appendix, page 90)

If the Certificate of Enthronement found on page 97 is used, it may be signed at this time.

OPTION B

ENTHRONEMENT DURING HOLY MASS

The Enthronement is to take place following the *Prayer After Communion*, at which time the congregation will process to the place of Enthronement.

The image of the Sacred Heart is to be blessed at the end of the intercessions. The following intercessions are recommended:

INTERCESSIONS

Priest: Lord Jesus, You told us that "whatever you ask the Father in my name, he will give to you." In Your name, and with great confidence in Your love, we now offer these prayers:

Someone other than the celebrant proposes the intercessions:

For the grace of being faithful to this covenant with Jesus and our renewed way of life in Him, let us pray:

R/. **Lord, hear our prayer.**

For an increase of personal, generous love for Jesus, and a greater trust in His merciful love, let us pray:

R/. **Lord, hear our prayer.**

That the Holy Spirit may always find our hearts responsive to His call, let us pray:

R/. **Lord, hear our prayer.**

For a deeper appreciation of the greatest gift of the Heart of Jesus, the Holy Eucharist, through frequent participation in the Holy Sacrifice of the Mass and Holy Communion, especially on First Fridays, let us pray:
R/. **Lord, hear our prayer.**

That we may desire to receive the Sacrament of Confession more often in order to increase our love for Jesus and to avoid sin, let us pray:
R/. **Lord, hear our prayer.**

That those who are absent may be protected in all they do, and that all our beloved who have died may be united to the Heart of Jesus in Heaven for ever, let us pray:
R/. **Lord, hear our prayer.**

BLESSING OF THE IMAGE

The image of the Sacred Heart is blessed by the priest. If an image of the Immaculate Heart of Mary is installed, the blessing found on page 81 may be used. If the images were previously blessed, the blessings are omitted at this time.

Priest:
Lord,
although Your glory lies beyond our sight,
out of Your great love
You have revealed Yourself in the Heart of Christ.
Bless ✠ this image of Your Son.
May those who venerate it
honor Christ by growing in His likeness,
Who is Lord for ever and ever.
R/. **Amen.**
The priest sprinkles the image with holy water.

ACT OF ENTHRONEMENT

Following the *Prayer After Communion,* a procession forms. An incense bearer, cross and candle bearers, the person carrying the image of the Sacred Heart, and a person carrying the Bible are followed by the priest and other ministers, then the members of the particular community. All process to the place of Enthronement. A hymn may accompany the procession.

When all arrive at the place of Enthronement, the priest enthrones the image of the Sacred Heart in the selected place saying:

I now enthrone Jesus as King and Friend of our *(parish, school, or other setting).*

The person carrying the Bible then places it near the image of the Sacred Heart and says:

We are nourished by the Body and Blood of Christ, and by the Word of God.

The candles are then placed on either side of the image as the candle bearers say together:

The Lord sits enthroned as King forever! *(Psalm* 29:10b) **All that the Lord has spoken we will do, and we will be obedient.** *(Exodus* 24:7)

If incense is used, the image is incensed.

ACT OF CONSECRATION

If possible, all kneel and say in unison:

To the Sacred Heart of Our Lord, Jesus Christ, we give ourselves and consecrate our lives, our actions, pains, and sufferings, so that we may be unwilling to make use of any part of our being other than to honor, love, and glorify Your Sacred Heart.

This is our unchanging purpose, namely, to be all Yours and to do all things for the love of You, at the same time renouncing with all our hearts whatever is displeasing to You. We therefore take You, O Sacred Heart, to be the only object of our love, the guardian of our lives, our assurance of salvation, the remedy of our weakness, the atonement for all our faults, and our sure refuge at the hour of death.

Be then, O Heart of goodness, our justification before God the Father. O Heart of love, we put all our confidence in You, for we fear everything from our own weakness and frailty, but we hope for all things from Your goodness and bounty.

Remove from us all that can displease You or resist Your Holy Will; let Your pure love imprint Your image so deeply upon our hearts that we shall never be able to forget You or to be separated from You.

May we obtain from Your loving kindness the grace of having our names written in Your Heart, for in You we desire to place all our happiness and glory, living and dying in You, Who live and reign with the Father and the Holy Spirit, one God, for ever and ever. Amen.

If an image of the Immaculate Heart of Mary is installed, the *Act of Consecration to the Immaculate Heart* found on page 82 is made at this point.

Priest: Let us conclude by calling on the Mother of God, Mary Most Holy:

HAIL HOLY QUEEN

All: **Hail, Holy Queen, Mother of Mercy, our life, our sweetness, and our hope! To thee do we cry, poor banished children of Eve; to thee do we send up our sighs, mourning and weeping in this valley of tears. Turn then, most gracious advocate, thine eyes of mercy toward us, and after this our exile, show unto us the blessed fruit of thy womb, Jesus. O clement, O loving, O sweet Virgin Mary.**

Priest: Pray for us, O holy Mother of God.
R/. **That we may be made worthy of the promises of Christ.**

Priest: Most Sacred Heart of Jesus,
R/. **have mercy on us.**

Leader: Immaculate Heart of Mary,
R/. **pray for us!**

Leader: Saint Joseph,
R/. **pray for us!**

Leader: Our Guardian Angels,
R/. **pray for us!**

Priest: Most Sacred Heart of Jesus,
R/. **have mercy on us.**

CLOSING PRAYER

Priest: Let us pray. O Father of mercies and God of all consolation, Who by the exceeding love with which You have loved us, have given us the Heart of Your beloved Son so that having but one heart with Him, we may love You perfectly, grant, we beseech You, that our hearts, being consumed in unity with the Heart of Jesus and with one another, may perform all our works in accord with His humility and charity and that, by His mediation, the just desires of our hearts may be accomplished, through the same Christ Our Lord.

R/. **Amen.**

BLESSING AND DISMISSAL

Priest: The Lord be with you.

R/. **And with your spirit.**

Priest: May almighty God bless you, the Father,
the Son, and ☩ the Holy Spirit.

R/. **Amen.**

Priest: Go in peace.

R/. **Thanks be to God.**

CLOSING HYMN

Holy God We Praise Thy Name (see Appendix, page 90)

If the Certificate of Enthronement found on page 97 is used, it may be signed at this time.

CHAPTER 7

CONSECRATION TO THE

Immaculate Heart of Mary

BLESSING OF THE IMAGE
OF THE IMMACULATE HEART

When the Immaculate Heart of Mary is installed, the image is to be blessed by a priest. The blessing is omitted at the time of Enthronement if the image has already been blessed.

Priest:
Lord, in the Blessed Virgin Mary
You have given Your pilgrim Church
an image of the glory to come.
Bless ✠ this image of the Blessed Virgin Mary,
Mother of Our Lord Jesus Christ.
Grant, we beseech Thee,
that those who honor her Immaculate Heart in this image
may humbly strive to serve and honor
Your only begotten Son, Our Lord Jesus Christ.
Through the intercession of the Blessed Virgin Mary,
may they gain from You grace in the present life and
eternal glory in the life to come, through Christ Our Lord.
R/: Amen.
The priest sprinkles the image with holy water.

ACT OF CONSECRATION
TO THE IMMACULATE HEART

All: **Most Holy Virgin Mary, tender Mother of men, to fulfill the desires of the Sacred Heart of Jesus and the request of the Vicar of your Son on earth, we consecrate ourselves and our families to your Sorrowful and Immaculate Heart, O Queen of the Most Holy Rosary, and we recommend to you, all the people of our country and all the world.**

Please accept our Consecration, dearest Mother, and use us as you wish to accomplish your designs in the world.

O Sorrowful and Immaculate Heart of Mary, Queen of the Most Holy Rosary, and Queen of the World, rule over us, together with the Sacred Heart of Jesus Christ, Our King. Save us from the spreading flood of modern paganism; kindle in our hearts and homes the love of purity, the practice of a virtuous life, an ardent zeal for souls, and a desire to pray the Rosary more faithfully.

We come with confidence to you, O Throne of Grace and Mother of Fair Love. Inflame us with the same Divine Fire which has inflamed your own Sorrowful and Immaculate Heart. Make our hearts and homes your shrine, and through us, make the Heart of Jesus, together with your rule, triumph in every heart and home. Amen. (Venerable Pope Pius XII)

Enthronement prayers continue on the following pages:
For Enthronement in the Home, page 42;
For Enthronement in Parishes, Schools and Other Settings
- ◆ *outside* of Holy Mass, page 70;
- ◆ *during* Holy Mass, page 79.

APPENDIX

O Sacred Heart of Jesus, formed by the Holy Spirit in the womb of the Virgin Mother, have mercy on us.

PRAYERS

Morning Offering to the Sacred Heart of Jesus

O Jesus, through the Immaculate Heart of Mary, I offer You my prayers, works, joys, and sufferings of this day in union with the Holy Sacrifice of the Mass throughout the world. I offer them for all the intentions of Your Sacred Heart: the salvation of souls, reparation for sin, the reunion of all Christians. I offer them for the intentions of our Bishops and of all Apostles of Prayer, and in particular for those recommended by our Holy Father this month. Amen.

Daily Prayer to the Sacred Heart

Dear Sacred Heart of Jesus, we renew our pledge of love and loyalty to You. Keep us always close to Your loving Heart and to the most pure Heart of Your Mother.

May we love one another more and more each day, forgiving each other's faults as You forgive us our sins. Teach us to see You in the members of our family and those we meet outside our home, and to love them, especially the poor and oppressed, that we may be instrumental in bringing about justice and peace.

Please help us to carry our cross daily out of love for You, and to strengthen this love by frequent Holy Mass and Holy Communion.

Thank You, dear Jesus, King and Friend of our family, for all the blessings of this day. Protect us and all families during this night. Help us so to live that we may all get to Heaven.

Most Sacred Heart of Jesus, have mercy on us.
Immaculate Heart of Mary, pray for us!
Saint Joseph, pray for us!
Our Guardian Angels, pray for us!
Most Sacred Heart of Jesus, have mercy on us.

Act of Renewal

This prayer, or the Act of Consecration on page 40, may be used to renew your Consecration on the Feast of the Sacred Heart, First Fridays, birthdays, anniversaries, or in times of sickness or death. It may also be used daily.

Most kind Jesus, humbly kneeling at Thy feet, we renew our Consecration to Thy Divine Heart. Be Thou our King forever! In Thee we have full and entire confidence. May Thy Spirit penetrate our thoughts, our desires, our words and our deeds. Bless our undertakings; share in our joys, in our trials and in our daily labors. Grant us to know Thee better, to love Thee more, to serve Thee without faltering.

By the Immaculate Heart of Mary, Queen of Peace, set up Thy Kingdom in our country. Enter closely into the midst of our families and make them Thine own through the solemn Enthronement of Thy Sacred Heart, so that soon one cry may resound from home to home: "May the triumphant Heart of Jesus be everywhere loved, blessed and glorified forever!" Honor and glory to the Sacred Hearts of Jesus and Mary.

Sacred Heart of Jesus, protect our families!
Most Sacred Heart of Jesus, Thy Kingdom come!
Immaculate Heart of Mary, pray for us!
Saint Joseph, friend of the Sacred Heart, pray for us!
Our Patron Saints and Guardian Angels, pray for us!

The Holy Rosary

The Joyful Mysteries

(Mondays, Saturdays, the Sundays of Advent, and Sundays from Epiphany until Lent)

1. The Annunciation of the Angel Gabriel to Mary *(Luke 1:26-38)*
2. The Visitation of Mary to Elizabeth *(Luke 1:39-56)*
3. The Birth of Our Lord *(Luke 2:1-20)*
4. The Presentation of the Infant Jesus in the Temple *(Luke 2:22-39)*
5. The Finding of the Child Jesus in the Temple *(Luke 2:41-52)*

The Luminous Mysteries

(Thursdays)

1. The Baptism of Jesus in the Jordan River *(Matthew 3:13-17)*
2. The Wedding Feast at Cana *(John 2:1-11)*
3. The Proclamation of the Kingdom of God
   (Mark 1:15, 2:3-12, Luke 7:47-48)
4. The Transfiguration of Jesus *(Matthew 17:1-8)*
5. The Institution of the Eucharist *(Matthew 26:26-29)*

The Sorrowful Mysteries

(Tuesdays, Fridays, and daily from Ash Wednesday until Easter Sunday)

1. The Agony of Jesus in the Garden *(Luke 22:39-46)*
2. The Scourging at the Pillar *(Mark 15:6-15)*
3. The Crowning with Thorns *(Matthew 27:28-31)*
4. The Carrying of the Cross *(Luke 23:26-32)*
5. The Crucifixion *(John 19:17-24)*

The Glorious Mysteries

(Wednesdays, and the Sundays from Easter until Advent)

1. The Resurrection of Jesus *(Matthew 28:1-10)*
2. The Ascension of Jesus *(Acts 1:6-11)*
3. The Descent of the Holy Spirit at Pentecost *(Acts 2:1-13)*
4. The Assumption of Mary into Heaven *(Revelation 11:19-12:1)*
5. The Coronation of Mary as Queen of Heaven and Earth
   (Revelation 12:1)

Litany of the Sacred Heart

Leader: Lord, have mercy.
R/. **Christ, have mercy.**
Leader: Lord, have mercy.

Leader: Christ, hear us.
R/. **Christ, graciously hear us.**

Leader: God, the Father of Heaven,
R/. **have mercy on us.** (repeat after each invocation)

Leader: God the Son, Redeemer of the world,
God the Holy Spirit,
Holy Trinity, one God,
Heart of Jesus, Son of the eternal Father,
Heart of Jesus, formed by the Holy Spirit in the womb
   of the Virgin Mother,
Heart of Jesus, substantially united to the Word of God,
Heart of Jesus, of infinite majesty,
Heart of Jesus, sacred temple of God,
Heart of Jesus, tabernacle of the Most High,
Heart of Jesus, house of God and gate of Heaven,
Heart of Jesus, burning furnace of charity,
Heart of Jesus, abode of justice and love,
Heart of Jesus, full of goodness and love,
Heart of Jesus, abyss of all virtues,
Heart of Jesus, most worthy of all praise,
Heart of Jesus, King and center of all hearts,
Heart of Jesus, in Whom are all the treasures
   of wisdom and knowledge,
Heart of Jesus, in Whom dwells the fullness of divinity,
Heart of Jesus, in Whom the Father was well pleased,

Heart of Jesus, of Whose fullness we have all received,
Heart of Jesus, desire of the everlasting hills,
Heart of Jesus, patient and most merciful,
Heart of Jesus, enriching all who invoke Thee,
Heart of Jesus, fountain of life and holiness,
Heart of Jesus, propitiation for our sins,
Heart of Jesus, loaded down with opprobrium,
Heart of Jesus, bruised for our offenses,
Heart of Jesus, obedient unto death,
Heart of Jesus, pierced with a lance,
Heart of Jesus, source of all consolation,
Heart of Jesus, our life and resurrection,
Heart of Jesus, our peace and reconciliation,
Heart of Jesus, victim for sin,
Heart of Jesus, salvation of those who trust in Thee,
Heart of Jesus, hope of those who die in Thee,
Heart of Jesus, delight of all the saints.

Leader: Lamb of God, Who takes away the sins of the world,
R/. **spare us, O Lord.**

Leader: Lamb of God, Who takes away the sins of the world,
R/. **graciously hear us, O Lord.**

Leader: Lamb of God, Who takes away the sins of the world,
R/. **have mercy on us.**

Leader: Jesus, meek and humble of Heart,
R/. **make our hearts like unto Thine.**

HYMNS

To Jesus Christ Our Sov'reign King

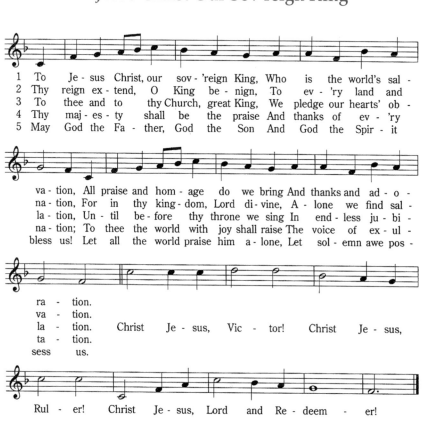

1 To Je - sus Christ, our sov - 'reign King, Who is the world's sal -
2 Thy reign ex - tend, O King be - nign, To ev - 'ry land and
3 To thee and to thy Church, great King, We pledge our hearts' ob -
4 Thy maj - es - ty shall be the praise And thanks of ev - 'ry
5 May God the Fa - ther, God the Son And God the Spir - it

va - tion, All praise and hom - age do we bring And thanks and ad - o -
na - tion, For in thy king - dom, Lord di - vine, A - lone we find sal -
la - tion, Un - til be - fore thy throne we sing In end - less ju - bi -
na - tion; To thee the world with joy shall raise The voice of ex - ul -
bless us! Let all the world praise him a - lone, Let sol - emn awe pos -

ra - tion.
va - tion.
la - tion. Christ Je - sus, Vic - tor! Christ Je - sus,
ta - tion.
sess us.

Rul - er! Christ Je - sus, Lord and Re - deem - er!

TEXT: Martin B. Hellriegel, 1890-1981, copyright © 1941 by Martin B. Hellriegel; assigned 1978 to Irene C. Mueller.
MELODY: *Mainz Gesangbuch*, 1870
HARMONIZATION: Calvert Shenk, b.1940, copyright © 1997 by Calvert Shenk

CHRISTUS REX (ICH GLAUB AN GOTT)
8 7 . 8 7 with Refrain

Holy God We Praise Thy Name

1 Ho - ly God, we praise thy name! Lord of
2 Hark! the loud ce - les - tial hymn An - gel
3 Lo! the Bless - ed Twelve pro - claim To the
4 Ho - ly Fa - ther, Ho - ly Son, Ho - ly

all, we bow be - fore thee. All on earth thy
choirs a - bove are rais - ing, Cher - u - bim and
Fa - ther hymns of glo - ry; Proph - ets sing in
Spir - it, Three we name thee; While in es - sence

scep - tre claim; All in heav'n a - bove a -
ser - a - phim In un - ceas - ing cho - rus
loud ac - claim; Mar - tyrs tell the won - drous
on - ly One, Un - di - vid - ed God we

dore thee. In - fi - nite thy vast do -
prais - ing, Fill the heav'ns with sweet ac -
sto - ry; And from morn to set of
claim thee; And a - dor - ing bend the

main, Ev - er - last - ing is thy reign.
cord: Ho - ly, Ho - ly, Ho - ly Lord.
sun, Through the Church they sing as one.
knee, While we own the mys - ter - y.

In - fi - nite thy vast do - main, Ev - er -
Fill the heav'ns with sweet ac - cord: Ho - ly,
And from morn to set of sun, Through the
And a - dor - ing bend the knee, While we

last - ing	is	thy	reign.
Ho - ly,	Ho - ly	Lord.
Church	they	sing	as	one.
own	the	mys - ter - y.	A - men.

TEXT: *Te Deum*, ascribed to St. Nicetas, ?-415,
    paraphrase translation by Clarence Augustus Walworth, 1820-1900, alt.
MELODY: from *Katholisches Gesangbuch*, Vienna 1774
HARMONIZATION: Anonymous

GROSSER GOTT (TE DEUM)
7 8 . 7 8 . 7 7 with Repeat

Immaculate Mary

1 Im - mac - u - late Mar - y, thy prais - es we sing,
2 In heav - en, the bles - sed thy glo - ry pro - claim;
3 Thy name is our pow - er, thy vir - tues our light,
4 We pray for our moth - er, the Church up - on earth;

Who reign - est in splen - dor with Je - sus our King.
On earth, we thy chil - dren in - voke thy fair name.
Thy love is our com - fort, thy plead - ing our might.
And bless, dear - est La - dy, the land of our birth.

Refrain

A - ve, A - ve, A - ve Ma - ri - a,

A - ve, A - ve Ma - ri - a.

TEXT: Anonymous
MELODY: Traditional French Cantique with Refrain added
HARMONIZATION: Calvert Shenk, b.1940, copyright © 1997 by Calvert Shenk

LOURDES HYMN
6 5 . 6 5 with Refrain

Litany of the Sacred Heart of Jesus

Lord, have mercy. **Christ, have mercy.** Lord, have mercy.
Christ, hear us. **Christ, graciously hear us.**
God the Father of Heaven: **have mercy on us.**
God the Son, Redeemer of the world: **have mercy on us.**
God, the Holy Spirit: **have mercy on us.**
Holy Trinity, one God: **have mercy on us.**

Refrain:

Jesus, meek and hum-ble of heart, make our hearts like___ un-to Thine.

Verses: Respond **"Have mercy on us"** to each invocation.

1. Heart of Christ, Son of the E-ter-nal Fa-ther: **have mer-cy on us;** formed by the Ho-ly Spi-rit: **have mer-cy on us;** in the womb of the Vir-gin: **have mer-cy on us;** U-nit-ed with the Word: **have mer-cy on us;** Heart of Christ, of In-fin-ite___ Maj-es-ty: **have mer-cy on us;** Ho-ly Tem-ple of God: **have mer-cy on us;** Tab-er-na-cle of the Most High: **have mercy on us;** House of God and Gate of Heaven: **have mercy on us.**
(to Refrain)

Text: Litany of the Sacred Heart, approved by Pope Leo XIII, 1899.
Tune: Dominican Sisters of St. Cecilia, © 2009, LBP Publications, Inc. Nashville, Tennessee. Used with permission. All rights reserved.

Verses 2, 3 and 4 continued on pages 93-95.

CONTINUED: Litany of the Sacred Heart of Jesus (verse 2)

2. Heart of Christ, Burning furnace of charity: have mercy on us; A-bode of justice and love: have mercy on us; Full of goodness and love: have mercy on us; A-byss of all virtues: have mercy on us; Heart of Christ, most worthy of all praise: have mercy on us; King and center of all hearts: have mercy on us; In whom dwell wisdom and knowledge: have mercy on us; In whom dwells fullness of divinity: have mercy on us. (to Refrain)

CONTINUED: **Litany of the Sacred Heart of Jesus (verse 3)**

3.Heart of Christ, in whom the Fa-ther was well - pleased: **have mer-cy on**
us; Of whose full-ness we've re - ceived: **have mer-cy on** us; De-sire of ev-er-last-ing
hills: **have mer-cy on** us; Most pa-tient and most mer-ci-ful: **have mer-cy on**
us; Heart of Christ, en-rich-ing all who call on Thee: **have mer-cy on**
us; Foun-tain of ho-li - ness: **have mer-cy on** us; Pro-pi - ti - a-tion for our
sins: **have mer-cy on** us; Load-ed down with op - pro-bri-um: **have mer-cy on**
us. **(to Refrain)**

Text: Litany of the Sacred Heart, approved by Pope Leo XIII, 1899.
Tune:Dominican Sisters of St. Cecilia, © 2009, LBP Publications, Inc. Nashville, Tennessee. Used with permission. All rights reserved.

CONTINUED: Litany of the Sacred Heart of Jesus (verse 4)

4. Heart of Christ, Bruised for our of-fen-ses: have mer-cy on us; O-be-di-ent to death: have mer-cy on us; Pierced with a lance: have mer-cy on us; Source of all con-so-la-tion: have mer-cy on us; Heart of Christ, our life and res-ur-rec-tion: have mer-cy on us; Peace and re-con-cil-i-a-tion: have mer-cy on us; Vic-tim for sin: have mer-cy on us; Sal-va-tion for man-kind: have mer-cy on us.

(to Refrain)

Text: Litany of the Sacred Heart, approved by Pope Leo XIII, 1899.
Tune: Dominican Sisters of St. Cecilia, © 2009, LBP Publications, Inc. Nashville, Tennessee. Used with permission. All rights reserved.

SOURCES / ACKNOWLEDGEMENTS

The Adoremus Hymnal. San Francisco: Ignatius Press, 1997. Used with permission.
Immaculate Mary, Hymn #532
To Jesus Christ, Our Sov'reign King, Hymn #480
Holy God We Praise Thy Name, Hymn #461

Catechism of the Catholic Church. Washington, D.C.: United States Catholic Conference, Inc., 1994.

Crawley-Boevey, Mateo. *Jesus King of Love.* Brewster, MA: Paraclete Press, 1997.

Diocese of La Crosse. *The Enthronement of the Sacred Heart Ceremonial for the Family.* La Crosse, WI: Office of Sacred Worship, 2003.

Larkin, Francis. *Enthronement of the Sacred Heart.* National Sacred Heart Enthronement Center, 2009.

Litany of the Sacred Heart of Jesus. Copyright © 2009 Dominican Sisters of Saint Cecilia. Used with permission. All rights reserved. May not be reproduced in any form without the permission of the Dominican Sisters of Saint Cecilia, Nashville, Tennessee.

O'Donnell, Timothy T. *Heart of the Redeemer.* Manassas, VA: Trinity Communications, 1989; reprint, San Francisco: Ignatius Press, 1992.

Sacred Heart of Jesus oil painting used throughout this document was produced by an unknown artist. The original oil painting hangs in the Archbishop's Residence in Saint Louis, Missouri.

Sacred Scripture quotations taken from the Revised Standard Version Catholic Edition of the Holy Bible.

Verheylezoon, Louis. *Devotion to the Sacred Heart.* Westminster, MD: The Newman Press, 1955.

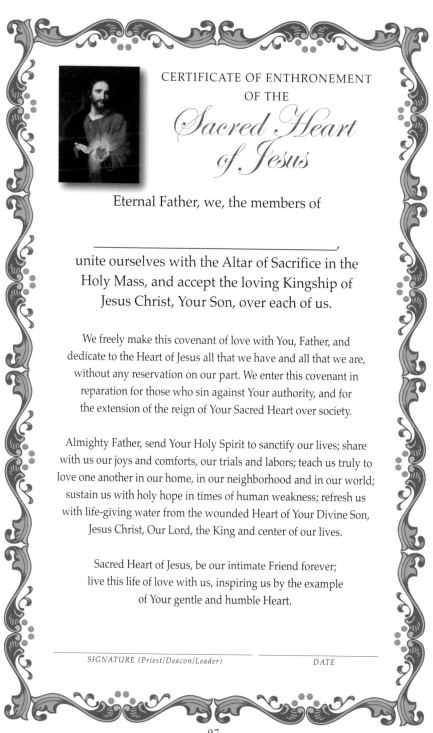

CERTIFICATE OF ENTHRONEMENT
OF THE

Sacred Heart
of Jesus

Eternal Father, we, the members of

_____,

unite ourselves with the Altar of Sacrifice in the
Holy Mass, and accept the loving Kingship of
Jesus Christ, Your Son, over each of us.

We freely make this covenant of love with You, Father, and
dedicate to the Heart of Jesus all that we have and all that we are,
without any reservation on our part. We enter this covenant in
reparation for those who sin against Your authority, and for
the extension of the reign of Your Sacred Heart over society.

Almighty Father, send Your Holy Spirit to sanctify our lives; share
with us our joys and comforts, our trials and labors; teach us truly to
love one another in our home, in our neighborhood and in our world;
sustain us with holy hope in times of human weakness; refresh us
with life-giving water from the wounded Heart of Your Divine Son,
Jesus Christ, Our Lord, the King and center of our lives.

Sacred Heart of Jesus, be our intimate Friend forever;
live this life of love with us, inspiring us by the example
of Your gentle and humble Heart.

_____   _____
SIGNATURE (Priest/Deacon/Leader)   DATE

CERTIFICATE OF ENTHRONEMENT
OF THE

Sacred Heart
of Jesus

NAMES OF THOSE IN ATTENDANCE

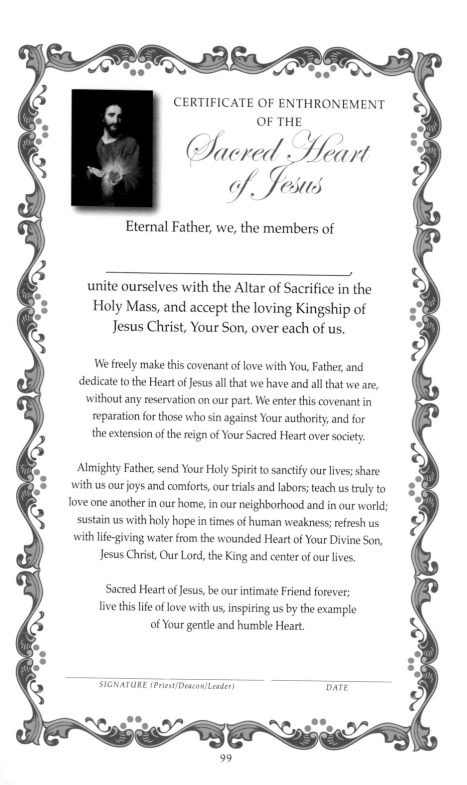

CERTIFICATE OF ENTHRONEMENT
OF THE

Sacred Heart of Jesus

Eternal Father, we, the members of

_____,

unite ourselves with the Altar of Sacrifice in the
Holy Mass, and accept the loving Kingship of
Jesus Christ, Your Son, over each of us.

We freely make this covenant of love with You, Father, and
dedicate to the Heart of Jesus all that we have and all that we are,
without any reservation on our part. We enter this covenant in
reparation for those who sin against Your authority, and for
the extension of the reign of Your Sacred Heart over society.

Almighty Father, send Your Holy Spirit to sanctify our lives; share
with us our joys and comforts, our trials and labors; teach us truly to
love one another in our home, in our neighborhood and in our world;
sustain us with holy hope in times of human weakness; refresh us
with life-giving water from the wounded Heart of Your Divine Son,
Jesus Christ, Our Lord, the King and center of our lives.

Sacred Heart of Jesus, be our intimate Friend forever;
live this life of love with us, inspiring us by the example
of Your gentle and humble Heart.

_____   _____

SIGNATURE (Priest/Deacon/Leader)   *DATE*

CERTIFICATE OF ENTHRONEMENT
OF THE

Sacred Heart
of Jesus

NAMES OF THOSE IN ATTENDANCE

_____

_____

_____

_____

_____

_____

_____

_____

_____

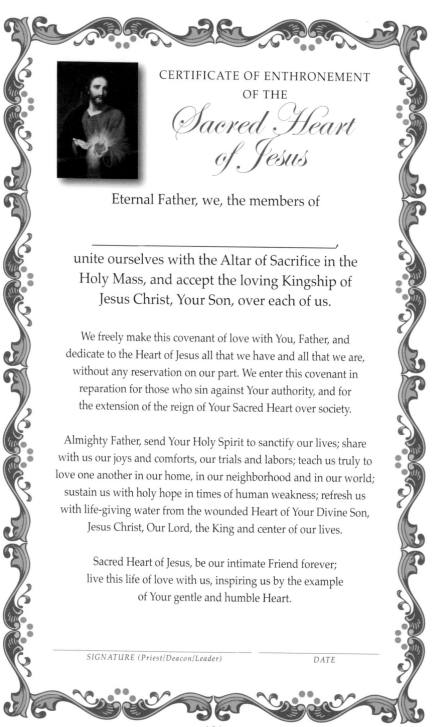

CERTIFICATE OF ENTHRONEMENT
OF THE

Sacred Heart
of Jesus

Eternal Father, we, the members of

_____,

unite ourselves with the Altar of Sacrifice in the
Holy Mass, and accept the loving Kingship of
Jesus Christ, Your Son, over each of us.

We freely make this covenant of love with You, Father, and
dedicate to the Heart of Jesus all that we have and all that we are,
without any reservation on our part. We enter this covenant in
reparation for those who sin against Your authority, and for
the extension of the reign of Your Sacred Heart over society.

Almighty Father, send Your Holy Spirit to sanctify our lives; share
with us our joys and comforts, our trials and labors; teach us truly to
love one another in our home, in our neighborhood and in our world;
sustain us with holy hope in times of human weakness; refresh us
with life-giving water from the wounded Heart of Your Divine Son,
Jesus Christ, Our Lord, the King and center of our lives.

Sacred Heart of Jesus, be our intimate Friend forever;
live this life of love with us, inspiring us by the example
of Your gentle and humble Heart.

_____   _____
SIGNATURE (Priest/Deacon/Leader)   DATE

CERTIFICATE OF ENTHRONEMENT
OF THE

Sacred Heart
of Jesus

NAMES OF THOSE IN ATTENDANCE

_____

_____

_____

_____

_____

_____

_____

_____

_____

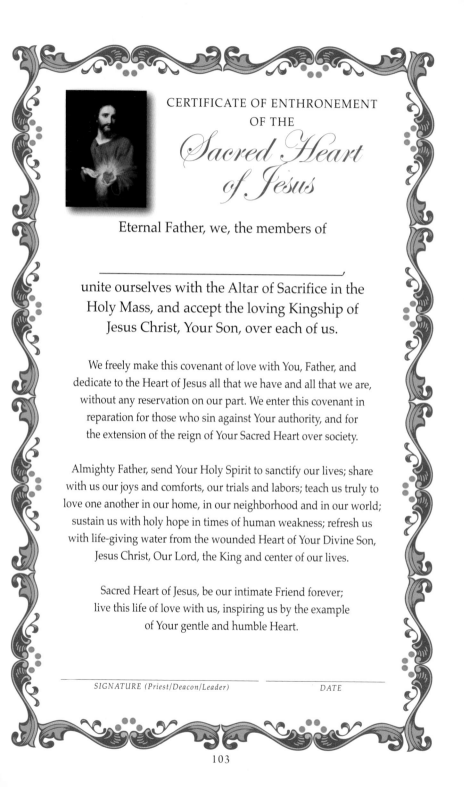

CERTIFICATE OF ENTHRONEMENT
OF THE

*Sacred Heart
of Jesus*

Eternal Father, we, the members of

_____,

unite ourselves with the Altar of Sacrifice in the
Holy Mass, and accept the loving Kingship of
Jesus Christ, Your Son, over each of us.

We freely make this covenant of love with You, Father, and
dedicate to the Heart of Jesus all that we have and all that we are,
without any reservation on our part. We enter this covenant in
reparation for those who sin against Your authority, and for
the extension of the reign of Your Sacred Heart over society.

Almighty Father, send Your Holy Spirit to sanctify our lives; share
with us our joys and comforts, our trials and labors; teach us truly to
love one another in our home, in our neighborhood and in our world;
sustain us with holy hope in times of human weakness; refresh us
with life-giving water from the wounded Heart of Your Divine Son,
Jesus Christ, Our Lord, the King and center of our lives.

Sacred Heart of Jesus, be our intimate Friend forever;
live this life of love with us, inspiring us by the example
of Your gentle and humble Heart.

_____   _____
SIGNATURE *(Priest/Deacon/Leader)*   *DATE*

CERTIFICATE OF ENTHRONEMENT
OF THE

Sacred Heart
of Jesus

NAMES OF THOSE IN ATTENDANCE

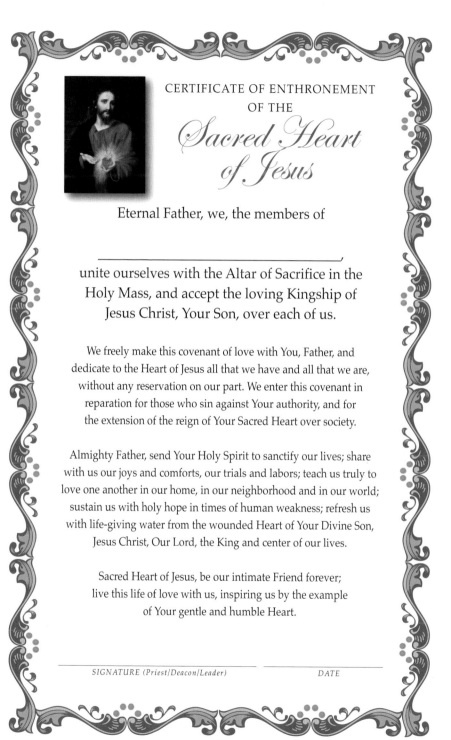

CERTIFICATE OF ENTHRONEMENT
OF THE

Sacred Heart
of Jesus

Eternal Father, we, the members of

_____,

unite ourselves with the Altar of Sacrifice in the
Holy Mass, and accept the loving Kingship of
Jesus Christ, Your Son, over each of us.

We freely make this covenant of love with You, Father, and
dedicate to the Heart of Jesus all that we have and all that we are,
without any reservation on our part. We enter this covenant in
reparation for those who sin against Your authority, and for
the extension of the reign of Your Sacred Heart over society.

Almighty Father, send Your Holy Spirit to sanctify our lives; share
with us our joys and comforts, our trials and labors; teach us truly to
love one another in our home, in our neighborhood and in our world;
sustain us with holy hope in times of human weakness; refresh us
with life-giving water from the wounded Heart of Your Divine Son,
Jesus Christ, Our Lord, the King and center of our lives.

Sacred Heart of Jesus, be our intimate Friend forever;
live this life of love with us, inspiring us by the example
of Your gentle and humble Heart.

_____   _____
SIGNATURE (Priest/Deacon/Leader)   DATE

CERTIFICATE OF ENTHRONEMENT
OF THE

Sacred Heart
of Jesus

NAMES OF THOSE IN ATTENDANCE